Copyright © 2005 Publications International, Ltd.
All rights reserved. This publication may not be reproduced in whole
or in part by any means whatsoever without written permission from

Louis Weber, C.E.O.
Publications International, Ltd.
7373 North Cicero Avenue
Lincolnwood, Illinois 60712

Ground Floor, 59 Gloucester Place
London W1U 8JJ

www.pilbooks.com

Permission is never granted for commercial purposes.

Manufactured in China.

8 7 6 5 4 3 2 1

ISBN 0-7853-7810-3

POEMS & PRAYERS

FOR CHILDREN

Written and compiled by Lynne Suesse

Illustrated by

Krista Brauckmann, Priscilla Burris, Lori Nelson Field,
Jennifer Fitchwell, Claudine Gévry, Kate Gorman, Linda Howard,
Elena Kucharik, Judy Love, Tammie Lyon, Babs McGuire, Laura Merer,
Kurt Mitchell, Marty Noble, Anne O'Connor, Christina Ong, Pam Peltier,
Judith Pfeiffer, Debbie Pinkney, Linda Prater, Karen Pritchett,
Tish Tenud, Anne Thornburgh, Rosario Valderrama

publications international, ltd.

Table of Contents

Thank You for the Morning Sun   5

My Family and Me   41

Mealtime Blessings   73

Following the Footsteps of Jesus   109

Jesus Loves Me   179

The World Around Me   225

Every Creature Great and Small   275

A Friend Is Love   307

Jesus loves every child.
And through His example,
children can learn to live,
and love, and grow.

Thank You for the Morning Sun

Each new day brings
the love of God.

For this new morning and its light,
For rest and shelter of the night,
For health and food, for love and friends,
For every gift Your goodness sends,
We thank You, gracious Lord.

I'll Be a Sunbeam

Jesus wants me for a sunbeam
  To shine for Him each day.
In every way try to please Him
  At home, at school, at play.

A sunbeam, a sunbeam,
  Jesus wants me for a sunbeam.
A sunbeam, a sunbeam,
  I'll be a sunbeam for Him.

O God, Creator of Light,

At the rising of Your sun this morning,

let the greatest of all light, Your love,

rise like the sun within our hearts.

Amen.

My Body, Strong and Good

I have two eyes that wink and blink,
  I have a mind to make me think,
I have two hands that clap for fun,
  I have two feet that jump and run,
I have two ears to hear a song,
  Two lips to praise Him all day long,
I have a body strong and good,
  To use for Jesus as I should.

When Morning Gilds the Skies

When morning gilds the skies,
My heart awaking cries:
May Jesus Christ be praised!
Alike at work and prayer
To Jesus I repair:
May Jesus Christ be praised!

Does sadness fill my mind?
A solace here I find:
May Jesus Christ be praised!
Or fades my earthly bliss?
My comfort still is this:
May Jesus Christ be praised!

I am small,
my heart is clean;
let no one dwell in it
except God alone.
Amen.

This morning, God,
this is Your day.
I am Your child.
Show me Your way.
Amen.

We Give Our Thanks

We give our thanks to Thee today,
　For Thou has blessed us in every way.
Help us to do the things we should,
　To be to others kind and good.

Lord Jesus Christ, be with me today,
And help me in all I think, and do, and say.

This is the day which the Lord has made;
let us rejoice and be glad in it.

Psalm 118:24

Hark! A Herald Voice Is Calling

Hark! a herald voice is calling,
"Christ is nigh," it seems to say.
"Cast away the dreams of darkness,
O ye children of the day!"

Wakened by the solemn warning,
Let the earth-bound soul arise.
Christ, her Sun, all sloth dispelling,
Shines upon the morning skies.

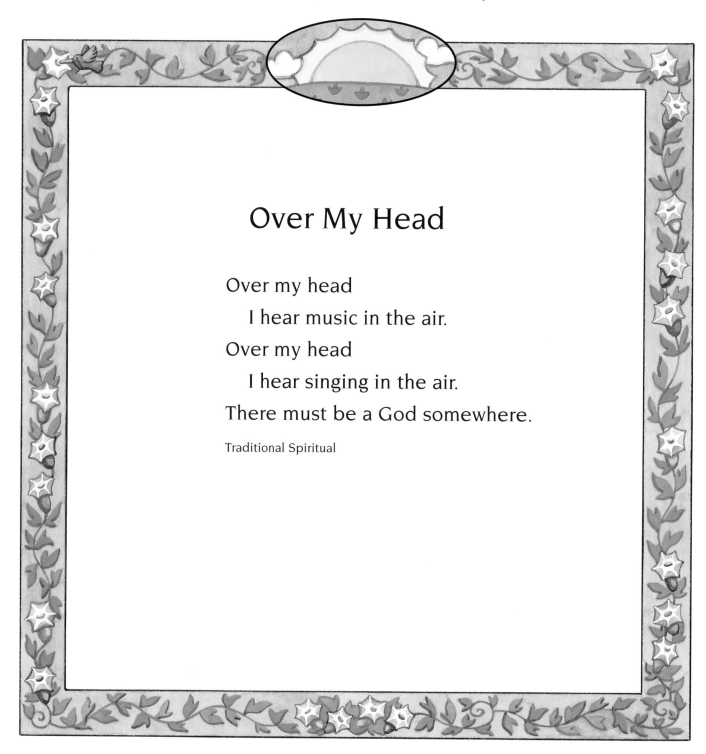

Over My Head

Over my head
   I hear music in the air.
Over my head
   I hear singing in the air.
There must be a God somewhere.

Traditional Spiritual

The year is at the spring
    And day is at the morn;
Morning is at seven;
    The hillside is dew-pearled;
The lark is on the wing;
    The snail is on the thorn;
God is in His heaven—
    All is right with the world.

Robert Browning

Good morning, Lord!

Be with me all day long,

until the shadows lengthen,

and the evening comes,

and the hustle and bustle of life is done,

and those at work are back at home.

Then in Thy mercy, grant us safe lodging,

and a Holy rest, and peace at the last.

Amen.

Do all the good you can,
   In all the ways you can,
In all the places you can,
   At all the times you can,
To all the people you can,
   As long as ever you can.

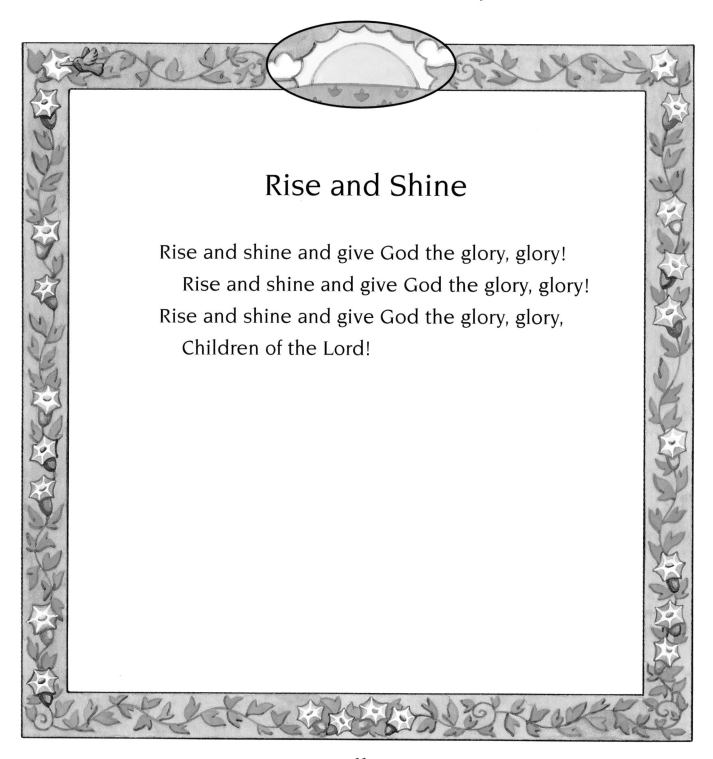

Rise and Shine

Rise and shine and give God the glory, glory!
Rise and shine and give God the glory, glory!
Rise and shine and give God the glory, glory,
Children of the Lord!

I have a busy day today, Jesus.
Help me to do my chores with cheer
and be kind to others,
even if they are not kind to me.
Watch over me as I walk the dog
and play with my friends.
Lord, I have a busy day.
Thank you for being by my side.

Amen.

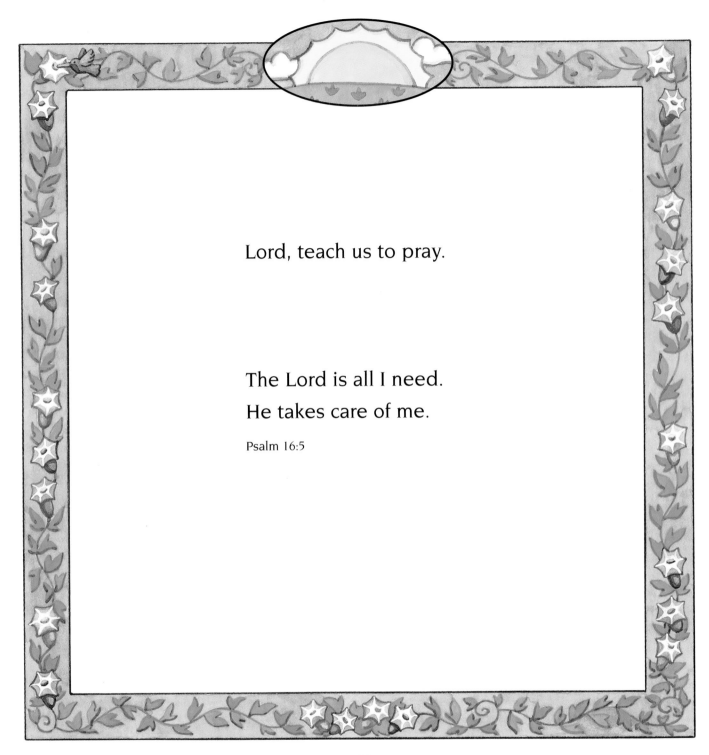

Lord, teach us to pray.

The Lord is all I need.
He takes care of me.

Psalm 16:5

How Brightly Beams
the Morning Star!

How brightly beams the morning star!
 What sudden radiance from afar
Doth glad us with its shining?
 Brightness of God, that breaks our night
And fills the darkened souls with light
 Who long for truth were pining!
Newly, truly, God's word feeds us,
 Rightly leads us,
Life bestowing.
 Praise, O praise such love overflowing!

Dear Father,

As we start this day, please guide us.

Please help Mom and Dad as they work.

Please help me at school.

Please help my little sister at home,

and all my other friends and family.

Amen.

My Family and Me

A family is God's way
of surrounding us with love.

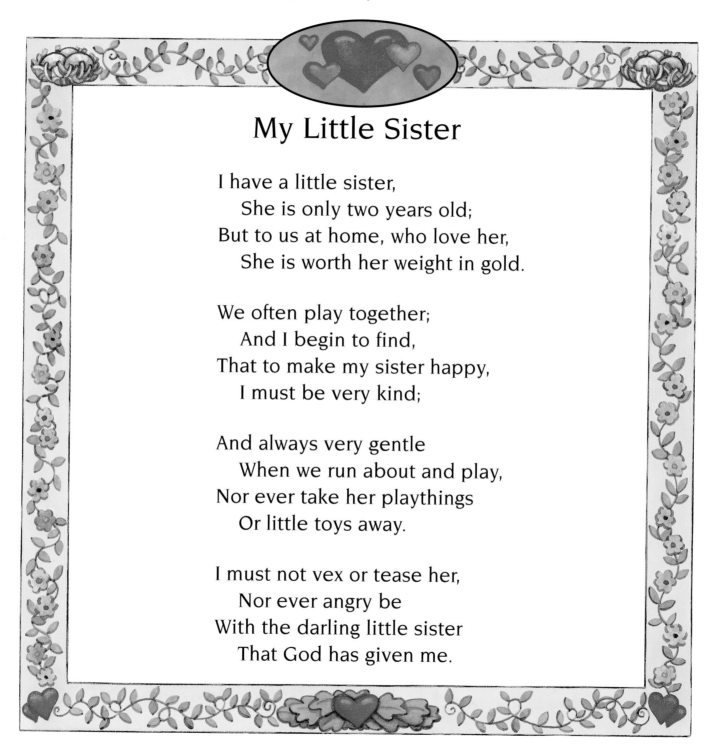

My Little Sister

I have a little sister,
    She is only two years old;
But to us at home, who love her,
    She is worth her weight in gold.

We often play together;
    And I begin to find,
That to make my sister happy,
    I must be very kind;

And always very gentle
    When we run about and play,
Nor ever take her playthings
    Or little toys away.

I must not vex or tease her,
    Nor ever angry be
With the darling little sister
    That God has given me.

I sought my soul,

But my soul I could not see.

I sought my God,

But my God eluded me.

I sought my brother,

And found all three.

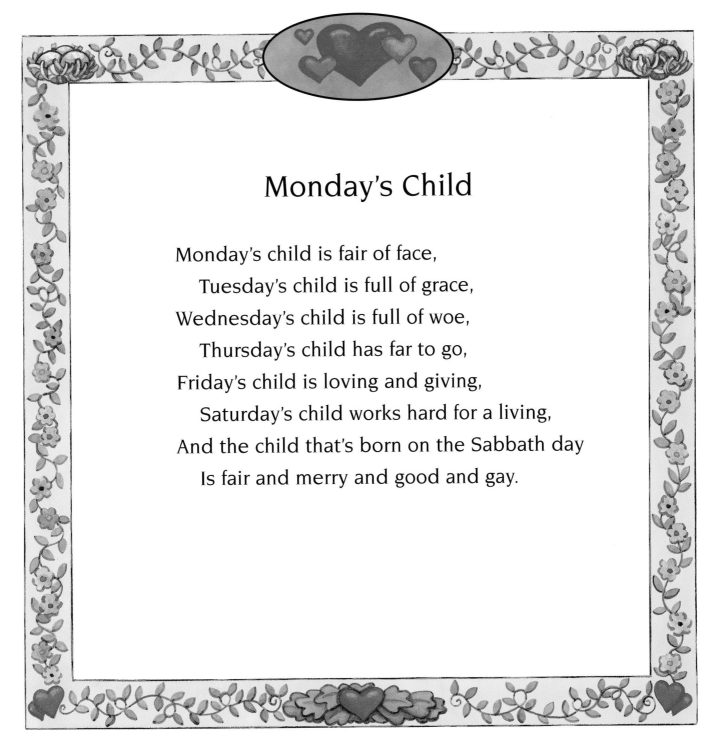

Monday's Child

Monday's child is fair of face,
   Tuesday's child is full of grace,
Wednesday's child is full of woe,
   Thursday's child has far to go,
Friday's child is loving and giving,
   Saturday's child works hard for a living,
And the child that's born on the Sabbath day
   Is fair and merry and good and gay.

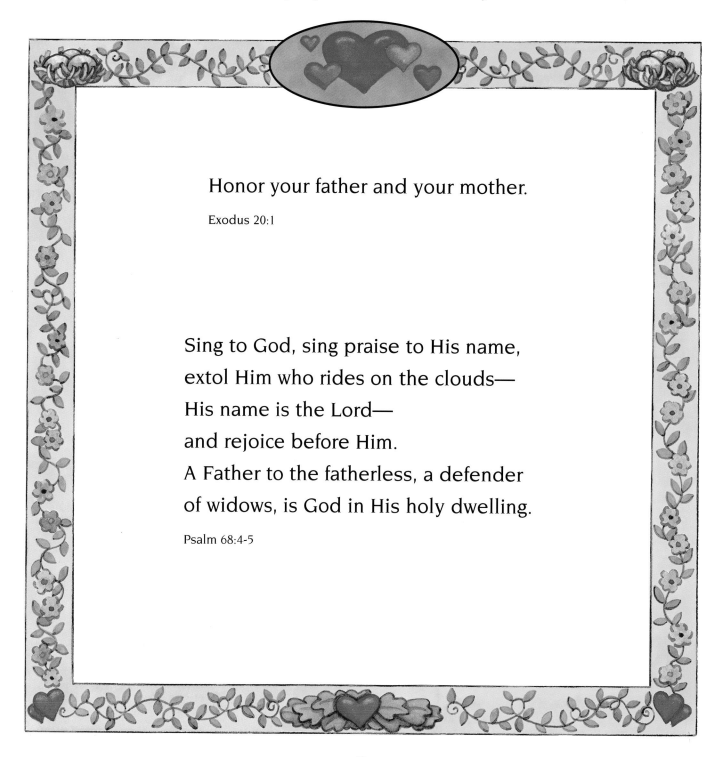

Honor your father and your mother.

Exodus 20:1

Sing to God, sing praise to His name,
extol Him who rides on the clouds—
His name is the Lord—
and rejoice before Him.
A Father to the fatherless, a defender
of widows, is God in His holy dwelling.

Psalm 68:4-5

I know that as I grow bigger
my love for my mother and father
will grow bigger, too.
Thank you, Jesus, for my parents.

Peace be to this house
and to all who dwell in it.
Peace be to them that enter
and to them that depart.

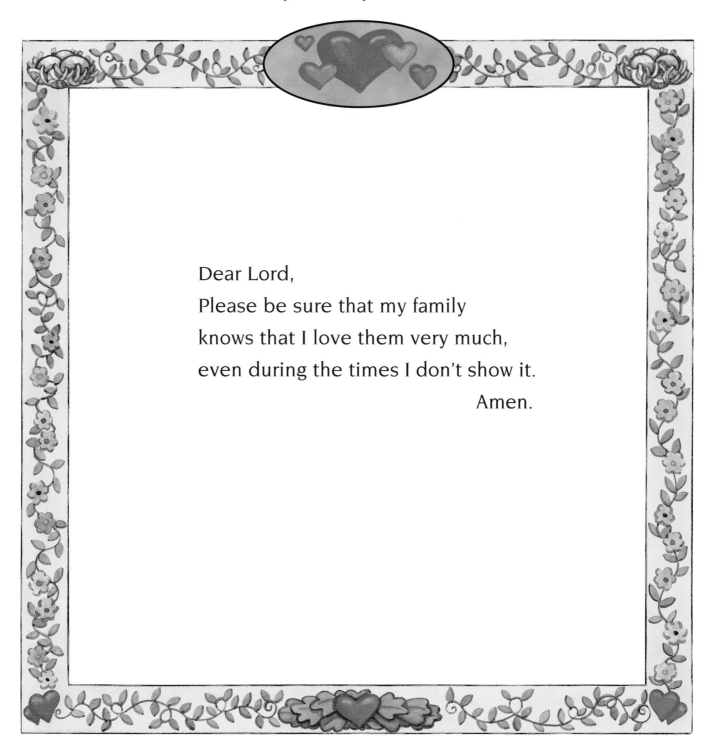

Dear Lord,

Please be sure that my family

knows that I love them very much,

even during the times I don't show it.

Amen.

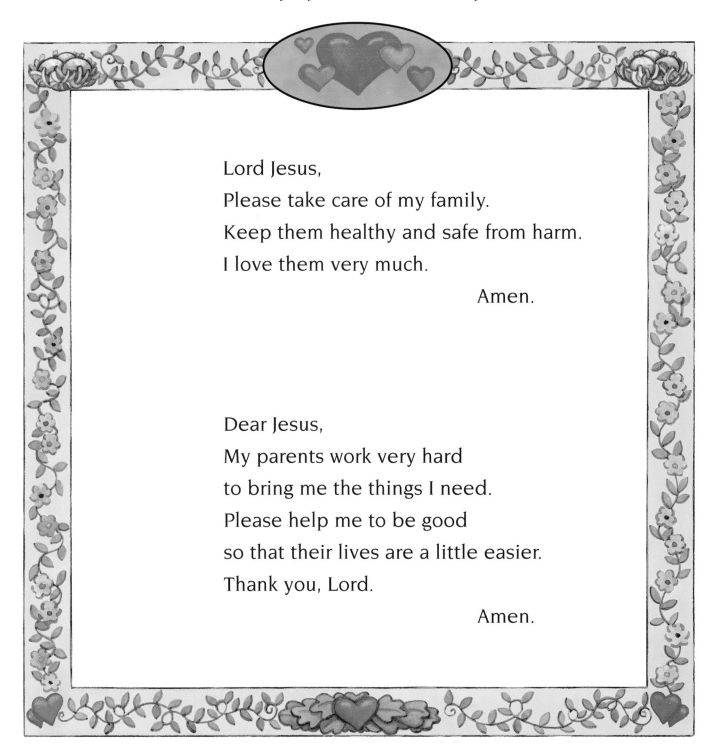

Lord Jesus,

Please take care of my family.

Keep them healthy and safe from harm.

I love them very much.

Amen.

Dear Jesus,

My parents work very hard

to bring me the things I need.

Please help me to be good

so that their lives are a little easier.

Thank you, Lord.

Amen.

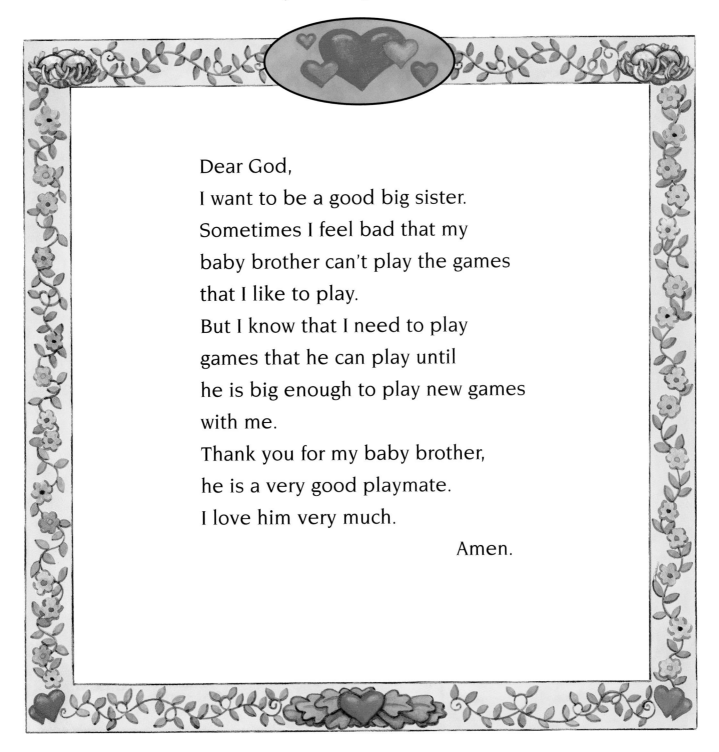

Dear God,
I want to be a good big sister.
Sometimes I feel bad that my
baby brother can't play the games
that I like to play.
But I know that I need to play
games that he can play until
he is big enough to play new games
with me.
Thank you for my baby brother,
he is a very good playmate.
I love him very much.

Amen.

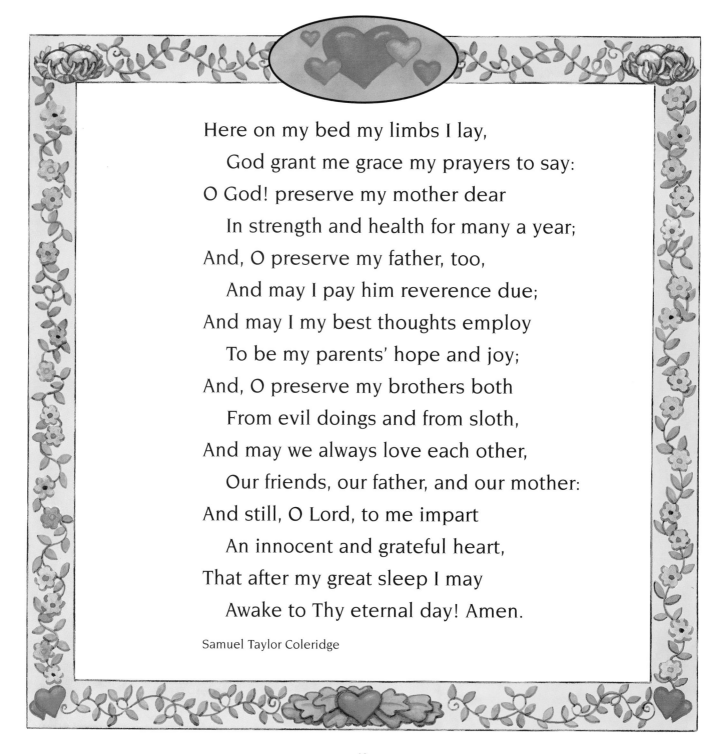

Here on my bed my limbs I lay,
God grant me grace my prayers to say:
O God! preserve my mother dear
In strength and health for many a year;
And, O preserve my father, too,
And may I pay him reverence due;
And may I my best thoughts employ
To be my parents' hope and joy;
And, O preserve my brothers both
From evil doings and from sloth,
And may we always love each other,
Our friends, our father, and our mother:
And still, O Lord, to me impart
An innocent and grateful heart,
That after my great sleep I may
Awake to Thy eternal day! Amen.

Samuel Taylor Coleridge

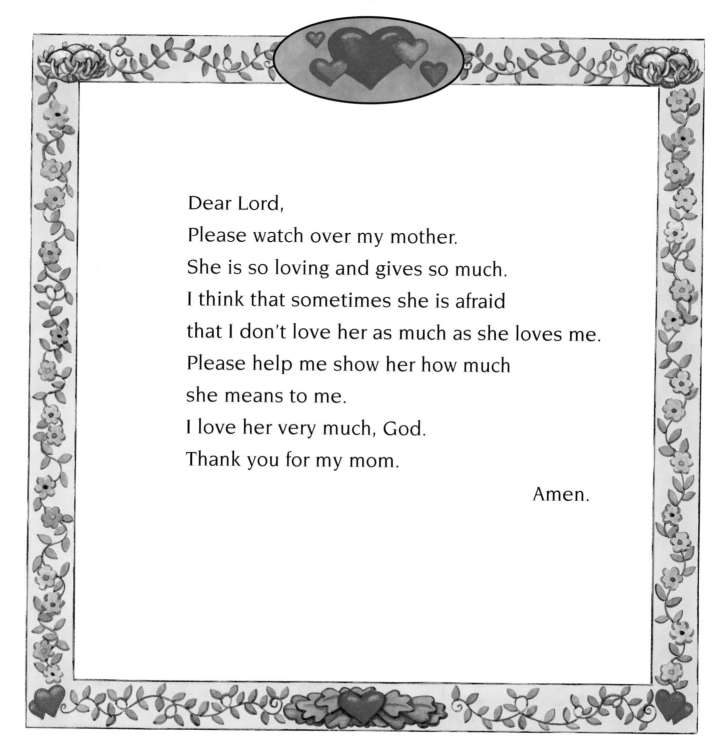

Dear Lord,

Please watch over my mother.

She is so loving and gives so much.

I think that sometimes she is afraid

that I don't love her as much as she loves me.

Please help me show her how much

she means to me.

I love her very much, God.

Thank you for my mom.

Amen.

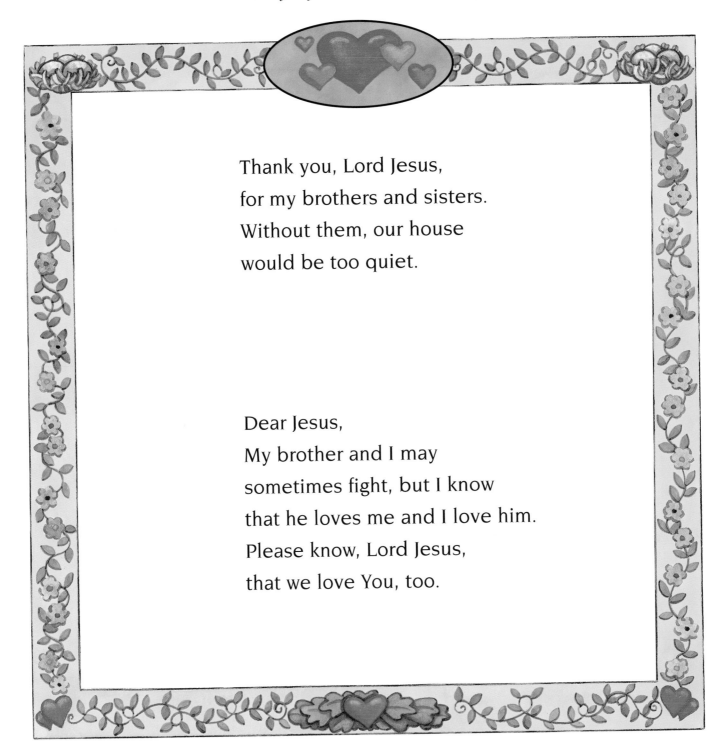

Thank you, Lord Jesus,
for my brothers and sisters.
Without them, our house
would be too quiet.

Dear Jesus,
My brother and I may
sometimes fight, but I know
that he loves me and I love him.
Please know, Lord Jesus,
that we love You, too.

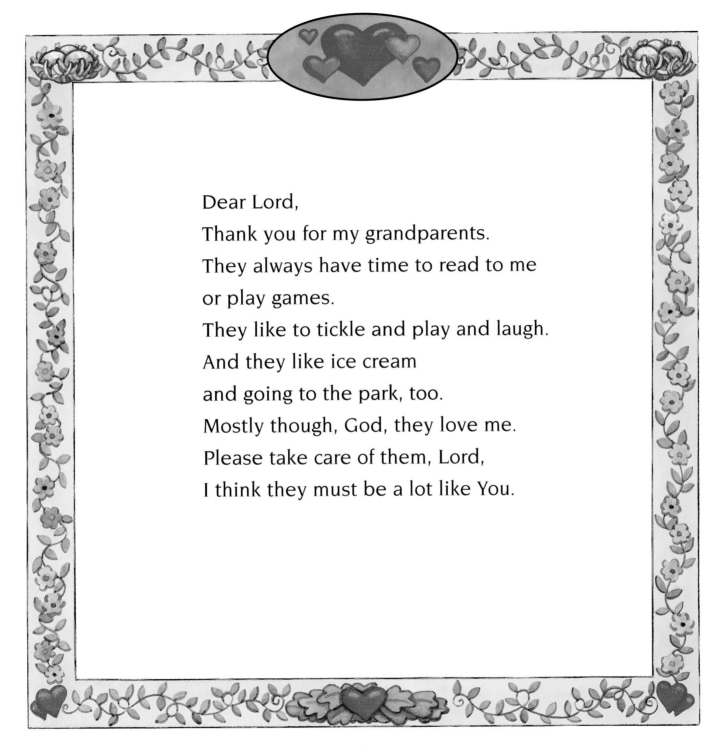

Dear Lord,

Thank you for my grandparents.

They always have time to read to me

or play games.

They like to tickle and play and laugh.

And they like ice cream

and going to the park, too.

Mostly though, God, they love me.

Please take care of them, Lord,

I think they must be a lot like You.

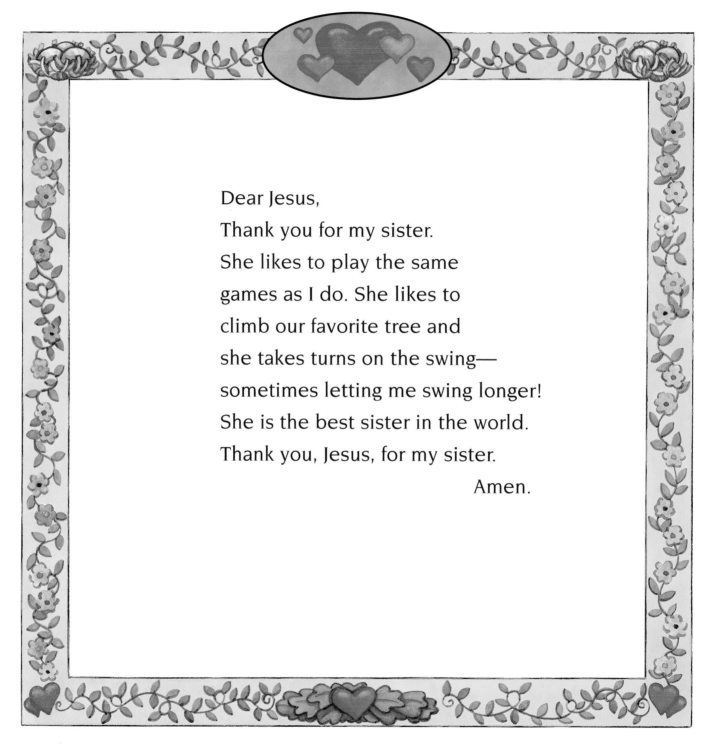

Dear Jesus,

Thank you for my sister.

She likes to play the same

games as I do. She likes to

climb our favorite tree and

she takes turns on the swing—

sometimes letting me swing longer!

She is the best sister in the world.

Thank you, Jesus, for my sister.

Amen.

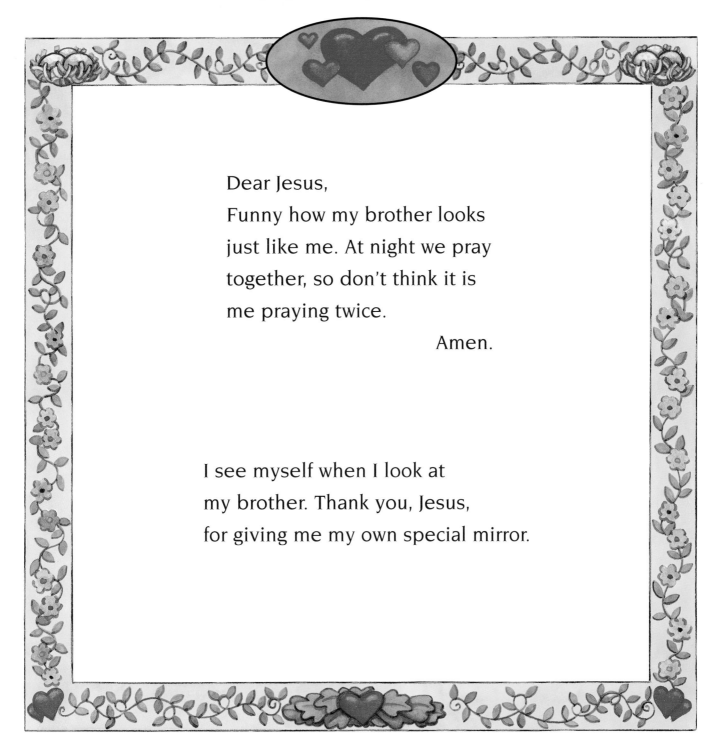

Dear Jesus,
Funny how my brother looks
just like me. At night we pray
together, so don't think it is
me praying twice.

                    Amen.

I see myself when I look at
my brother. Thank you, Jesus,
for giving me my own special mirror.

God bless all those that I love.

God bless all those that love me.

God bless all those that love those that I love,

And all those that love those who love me.

Mealtime Blessings

A blessing at mealtime is the perfect
way to say, "Thank you, God."

Our Hands We Fold

Our hands we fold,
    Our heads we bow,
For food and drink
    We thank Thee now.

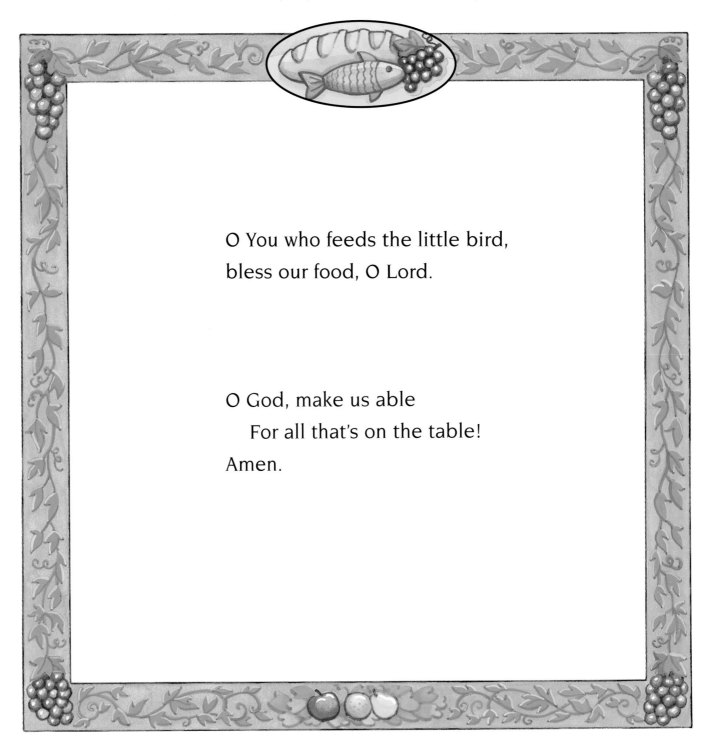

O You who feeds the little bird,
bless our food, O Lord.

O God, make us able
   For all that's on the table!
Amen.

We thank Thee, Lord,
　　For happy hearts,
　For rain and sunny weather;
　　We thank Thee, Lord,
For this our food,
　　And that we are together.

God is great,
　　God is good,
And we thank Him
　　For our food.
Amen.

It is very nice to think
   The world is full of meat and drink,
With little children saying grace
   In every Christian kind of place.

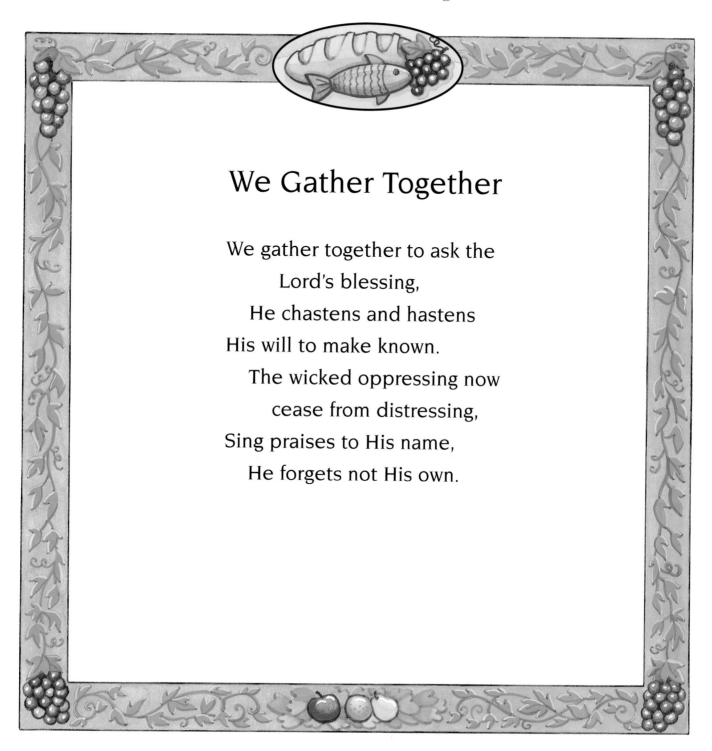

We Gather Together

We gather together to ask the
Lord's blessing,
He chastens and hastens
His will to make known.
The wicked oppressing now
cease from distressing,
Sing praises to His name,
He forgets not His own.

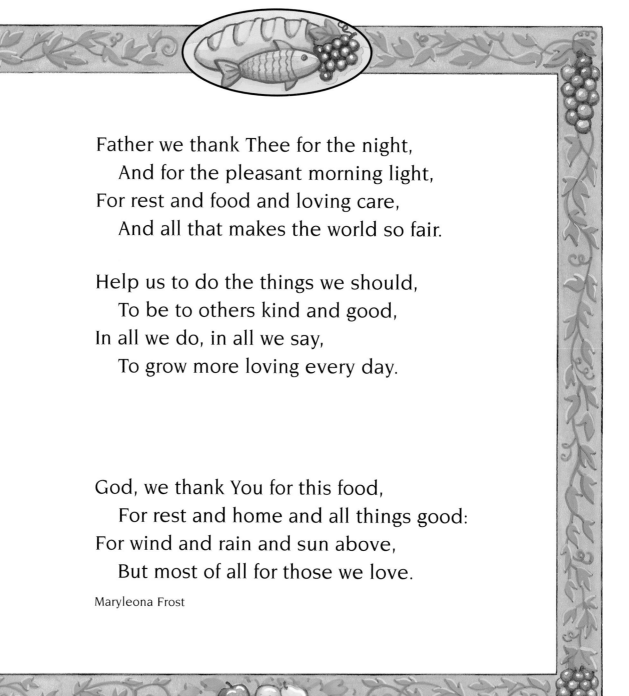

Father we thank Thee for the night,
　And for the pleasant morning light,
For rest and food and loving care,
　And all that makes the world so fair.

Help us to do the things we should,
　To be to others kind and good,
In all we do, in all we say,
　To grow more loving every day.

God, we thank You for this food,
　For rest and home and all things good:
For wind and rain and sun above,
　But most of all for those we love.

Maryleona Frost

Bless Thou the Gifts

Bless Thou the gifts our hands have brought;
    Bless Thou the work our hearts have planned.
Ours is the faith, the will, the thought;
    The rest, O God, is in Thy hand.
Amen.

    Come, Lord Jesus,
        Be our guest.
    Let these gifts
        To us be blessed.

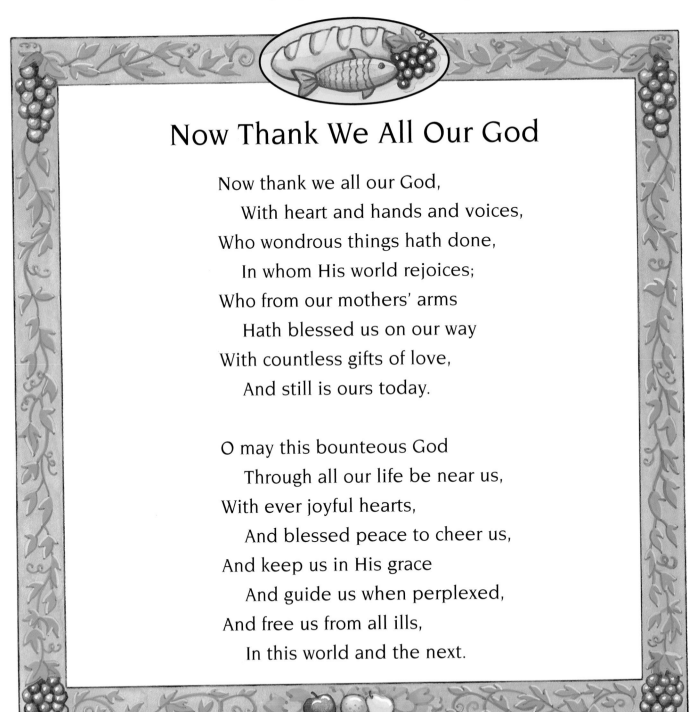

Now Thank We All Our God

Now thank we all our God,
    With heart and hands and voices,
Who wondrous things hath done,
    In whom His world rejoices;
Who from our mothers' arms
    Hath blessed us on our way
With countless gifts of love,
    And still is ours today.

O may this bounteous God
    Through all our life be near us,
With ever joyful hearts,
    And blessed peace to cheer us,
And keep us in His grace
    And guide us when perplexed,
And free us from all ills,
    In this world and the next.

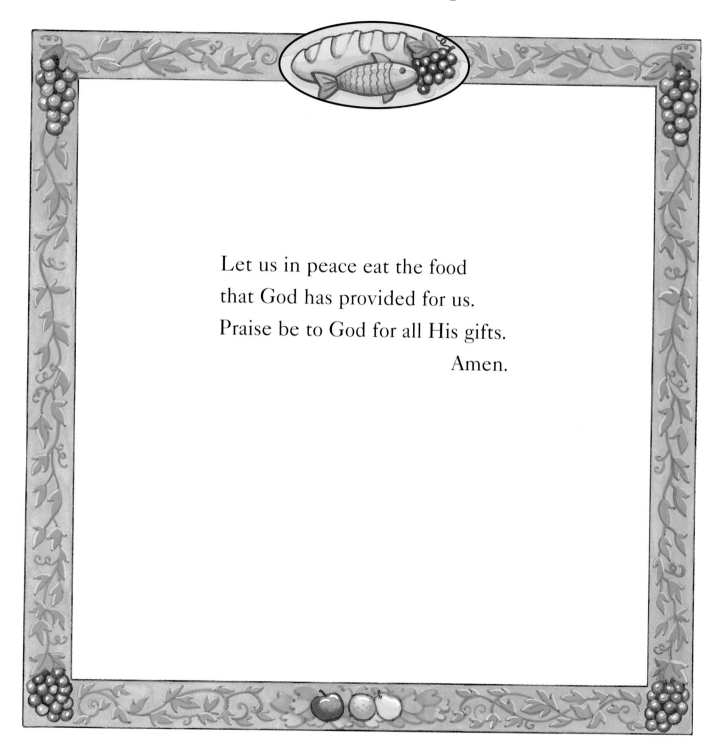

Let us in peace eat the food
that God has provided for us.
Praise be to God for all His gifts.
Amen.

Thank you for the world so sweet,
Thank you for the food we eat.
Thank you for the birds that sing,
Thank you, God, for everything.

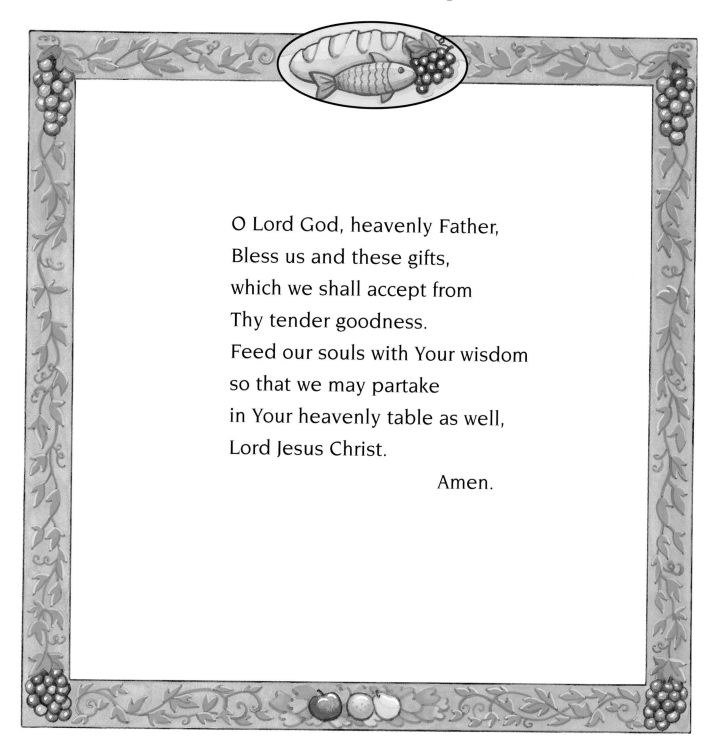

O Lord God, heavenly Father,
Bless us and these gifts,
which we shall accept from
Thy tender goodness.
Feed our souls with Your wisdom
so that we may partake
in Your heavenly table as well,
Lord Jesus Christ.

Amen.

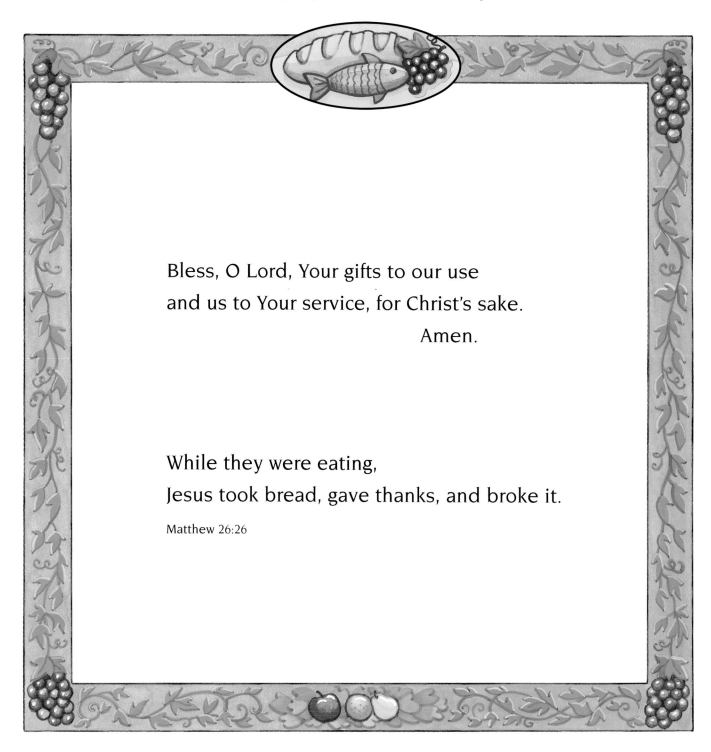

Bless, O Lord, Your gifts to our use
and us to Your service, for Christ's sake.

Amen.

While they were eating,
Jesus took bread, gave thanks, and broke it.

Matthew 26:26

We Plough the Fields, and Scatter

We plough the fields, and scatter
  The good seed on the land,
But it is fed and watered
  By God's almighty hand:
He sends the snow in winter,
  The warmth to swell the grain,
The breezes and the sunshine,
  And soft refreshing rain.

All good gifts around us
  Are sent from heaven above;
Then thank the Lord,
  O thank the Lord,
For all His love.

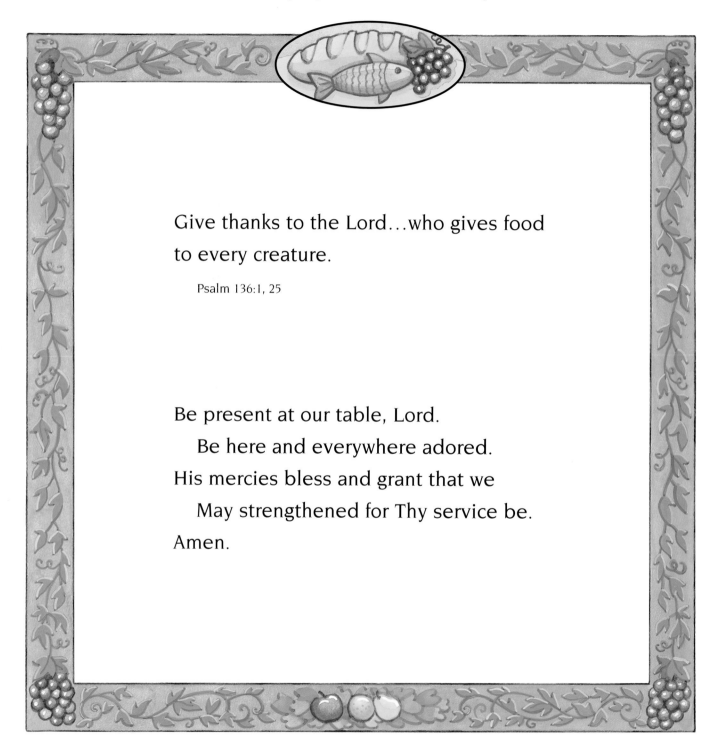

Give thanks to the Lord…who gives food
to every creature.

Psalm 136:1, 25

Be present at our table, Lord.
    Be here and everywhere adored.
His mercies bless and grant that we
    May strengthened for Thy service be.
Amen.

For every cup and plateful,
God, make us truly grateful!

Each time we eat,
may we remember
God's love.
Amen.

Come, Ye Thankful People

Come, ye thankful people, come—
 Raise the song of harvest home.
All is safely gathered in
 Ere the winter storms begin.
God, our Maker, doth provide
 For our wants to be supplied.
Come to God's own temple, come—
 Raise the song of harvest home.

All the world is God's own field,
 Fruit unto His praise to yield.
Wheat and tares together sown,
 Unto joy or sorrow grown.
First the blade and then the ear,
 Then the full corn shall appear.
Lord of harvest, grant that we
 Wholesome grain and pure may be.

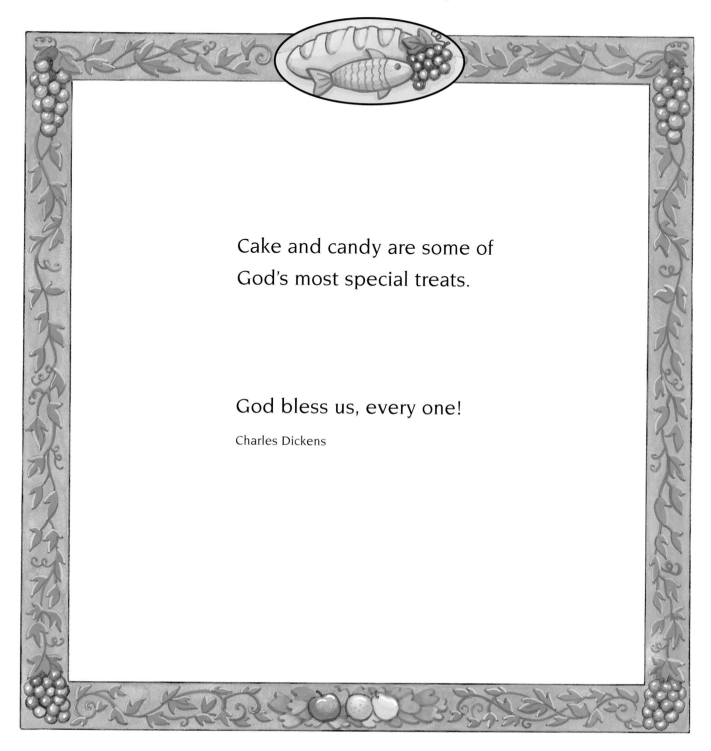

Cake and candy are some of
God's most special treats.

God bless us, every one!

Charles Dickens

Thank you, O Lord,
for Thy gifts which
we are about to receive
from Thy bounty.

Amen.

Following the Footsteps of Jesus

The lessons of life are found
in the love of Jesus.

The Wind Tells Me

The wind tells me,
   The birds tell me,
The Bible tells me, too,
   How much our Father loves us all,
And now I'm telling you.

It's Me, O Lord

It's me, it's me, it's me, O Lord,
   Standing in the need of prayer.
It's me, it's me, O Lord,
   Standing in the need of prayer.

Not my brother or my sister,
   But it's me, O Lord,
Standing in the need of prayer.
   Not my brother or my sister,
But it's me, O Lord,
   Standing in the need of prayer.

'Tis the gift to be simple,
'Tis the gift to be free,
'Tis the gift to come down
Where we ought to be.
And when we find ourselves
In the place just right,
'Twill be in the valley
Of love and delight.
When true simplicity is gained,
To bow and to bend,
We shall not be ashamed.
To turn, turn will be our delight
Till by turning, turning,
We come out right.

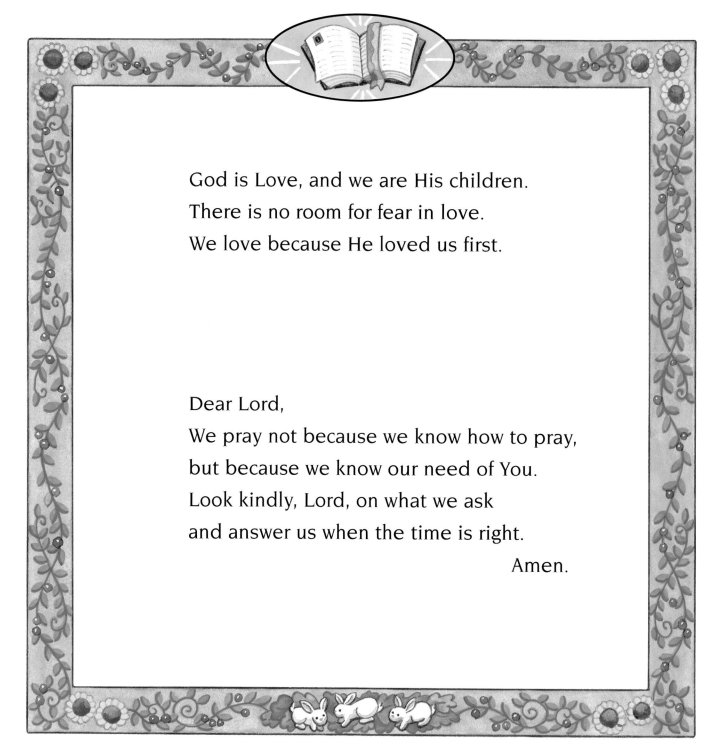

God is Love, and we are His children.

There is no room for fear in love.

We love because He loved us first.

Dear Lord,

We pray not because we know how to pray,

but because we know our need of You.

Look kindly, Lord, on what we ask

and answer us when the time is right.

Amen.

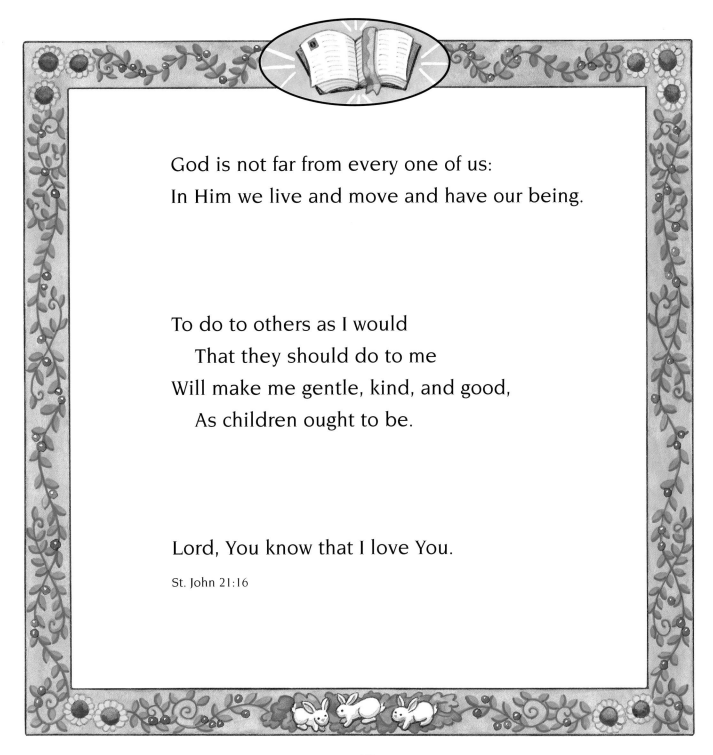

God is not far from every one of us:

In Him we live and move and have our being.

To do to others as I would

   That they should do to me

Will make me gentle, kind, and good,

   As children ought to be.

Lord, You know that I love You.

St. John 21:16

The Bible Says

The Bible says that Jesus
  Was loving, kind, and good.
I want to live as Jesus did,
  And do the things I should.

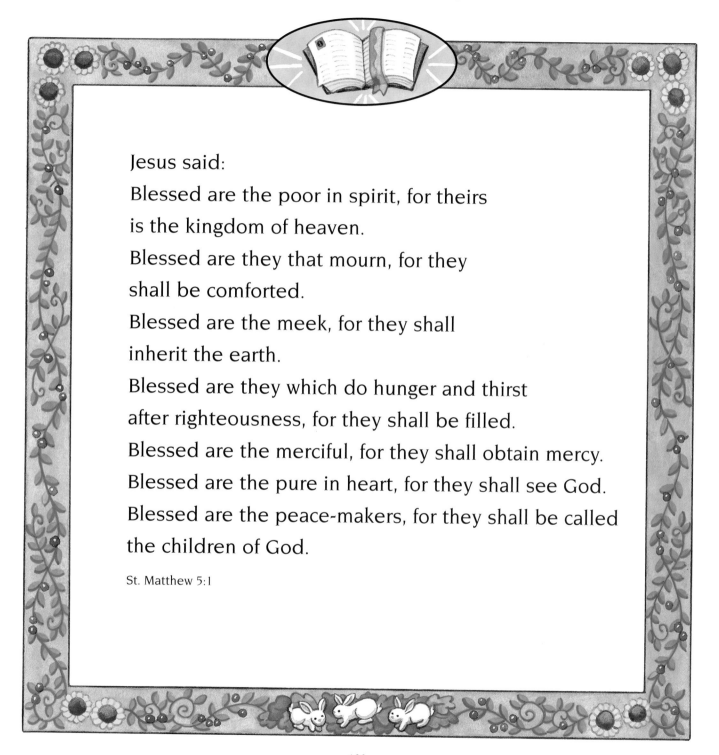

Jesus said:

Blessed are the poor in spirit, for theirs
is the kingdom of heaven.

Blessed are they that mourn, for they
shall be comforted.

Blessed are the meek, for they shall
inherit the earth.

Blessed are they which do hunger and thirst
after righteousness, for they shall be filled.

Blessed are the merciful, for they shall obtain mercy.

Blessed are the pure in heart, for they shall see God.

Blessed are the peace-makers, for they shall be called
the children of God.

St. Matthew 5:1

When I pray I speak to God,

when I listen God speaks to me.

I am now in His presence.

He is very near to me.

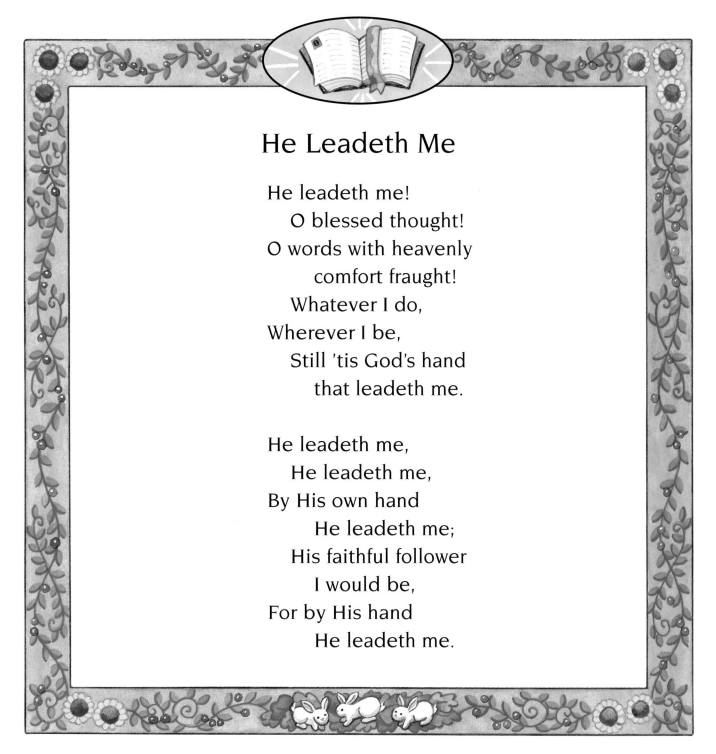

He Leadeth Me

He leadeth me!
   O blessed thought!
O words with heavenly
   comfort fraught!
Whatever I do,
Wherever I be,
   Still 'tis God's hand
     that leadeth me.

He leadeth me,
   He leadeth me,
By His own hand
   He leadeth me;
   His faithful follower
   I would be,
For by His hand
   He leadeth me.

Take Time to Be Holy

Take time to be holy,
    Speak often with thy Lord;
Abide in Him always
    And feed on His word.
Make friends of God's children,
    Help those who are weak,
Forgetting in nothing
    His blessing to seek.

Take time to be holy,
    The world rushes on;
Spend much time in secret
    With Jesus alone.
By looking to Jesus,
    Like Him thou shalt be;
Thy friends in thy conduct
    His likeness shall see.

Kind Deeds

Little drops of water,
  Little grains of sand,
Make the mighty ocean,
  And the pleasant land.

Thus the little minutes,
  Humble though they be,
Make the mighty ages
  Of eternity.

Little deeds of kindness,
  Little words of love,
Make this earth an Eden
  Like the heaven above.

Isaac Watts

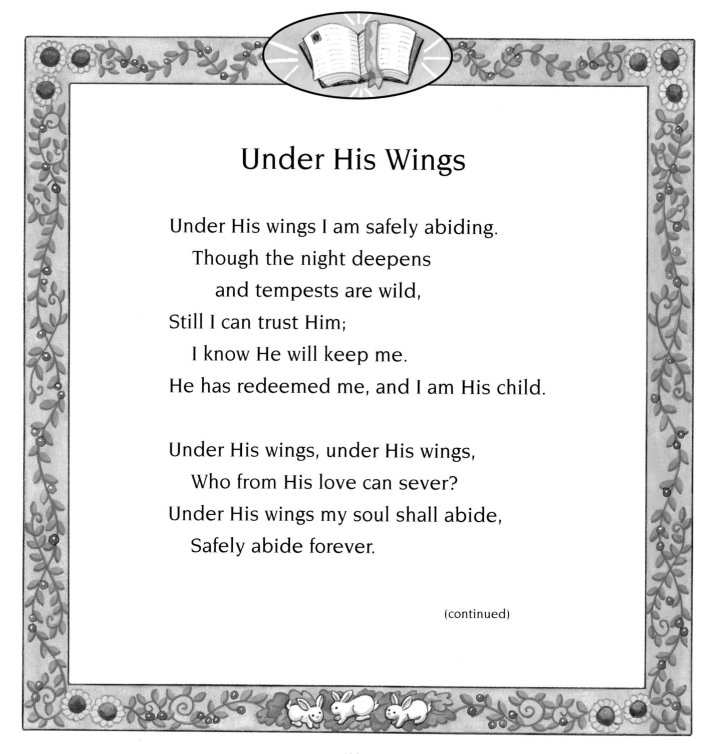

Under His Wings

Under His wings I am safely abiding.
　Though the night deepens
　　and tempests are wild,
Still I can trust Him;
　I know He will keep me.
He has redeemed me, and I am His child.

Under His wings, under His wings,
　Who from His love can sever?
Under His wings my soul shall abide,
　Safely abide forever.

(continued)

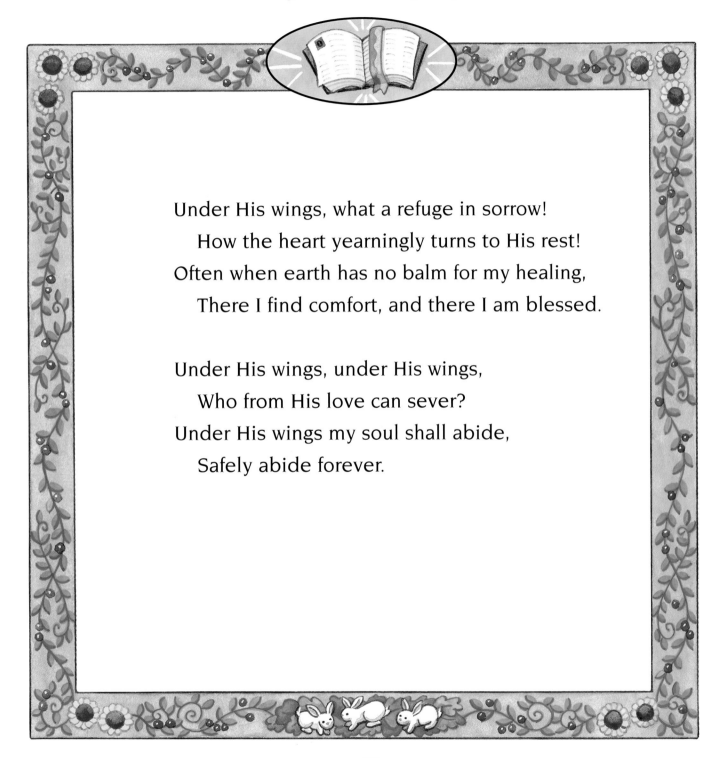

Under His wings, what a refuge in sorrow!
How the heart yearningly turns to His rest!
Often when earth has no balm for my healing,
There I find comfort, and there I am blessed.

Under His wings, under His wings,
Who from His love can sever?
Under His wings my soul shall abide,
Safely abide forever.

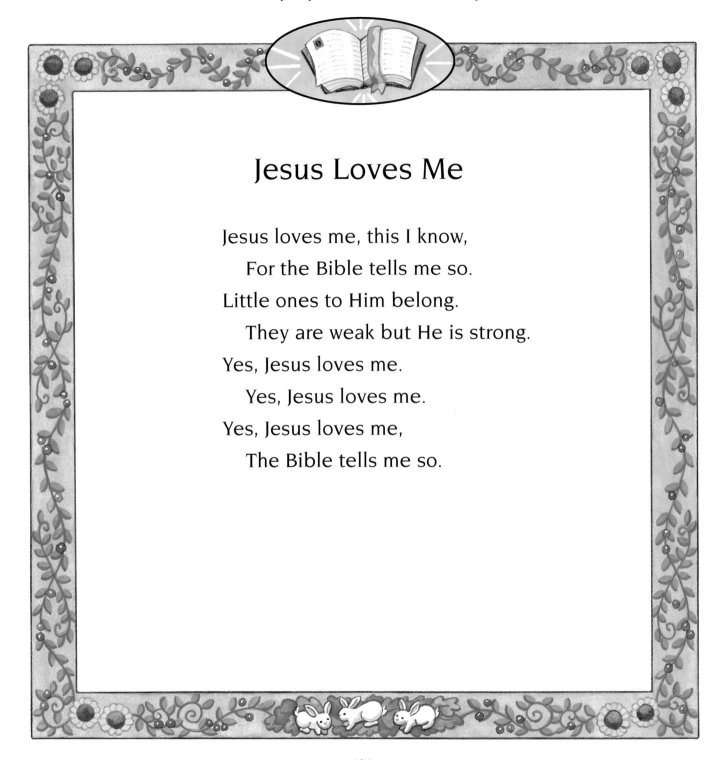

Jesus Loves Me

Jesus loves me, this I know,

    For the Bible tells me so.

Little ones to Him belong.

    They are weak but He is strong.

Yes, Jesus loves me.

    Yes, Jesus loves me.

Yes, Jesus loves me,

    The Bible tells me so.

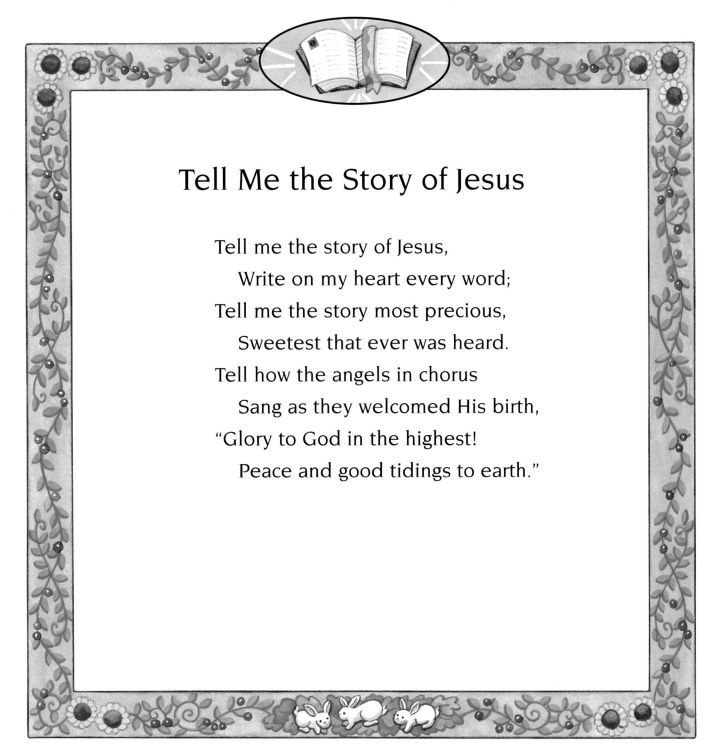

Tell Me the Story of Jesus

Tell me the story of Jesus,
    Write on my heart every word;
Tell me the story most precious,
    Sweetest that ever was heard.
Tell how the angels in chorus
    Sang as they welcomed His birth,
"Glory to God in the highest!
    Peace and good tidings to earth."

Lord, since You exist, we exist.

Since You are beautiful,

we are beautiful.

Since You are good,

we are good.

By our existence we honor You.

By our beauty we glorify You.

By our goodness we love You.

Edmund of Abington

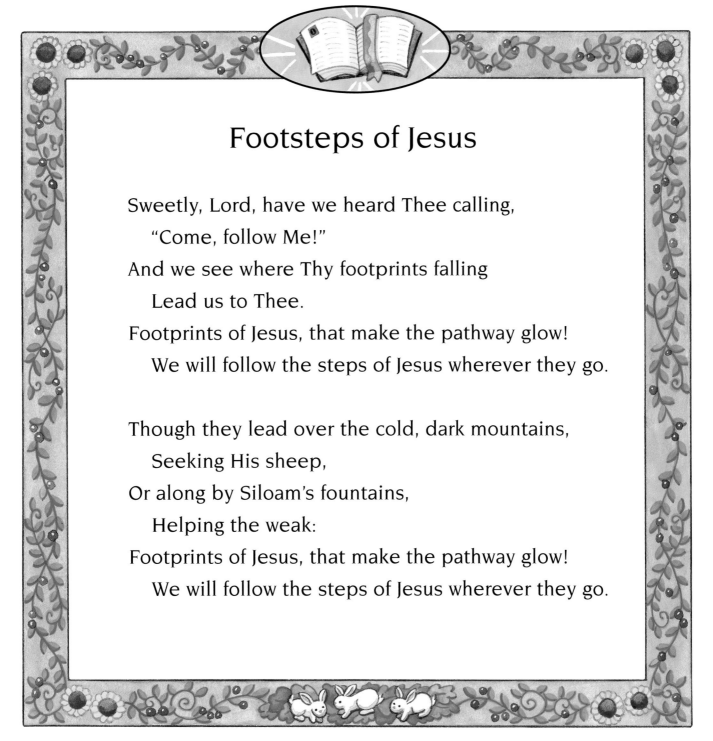

Footsteps of Jesus

Sweetly, Lord, have we heard Thee calling,
    "Come, follow Me!"
And we see where Thy footprints falling
    Lead us to Thee.
Footprints of Jesus, that make the pathway glow!
    We will follow the steps of Jesus wherever they go.

Though they lead over the cold, dark mountains,
    Seeking His sheep,
Or along by Siloam's fountains,
    Helping the weak:
Footprints of Jesus, that make the pathway glow!
    We will follow the steps of Jesus wherever they go.

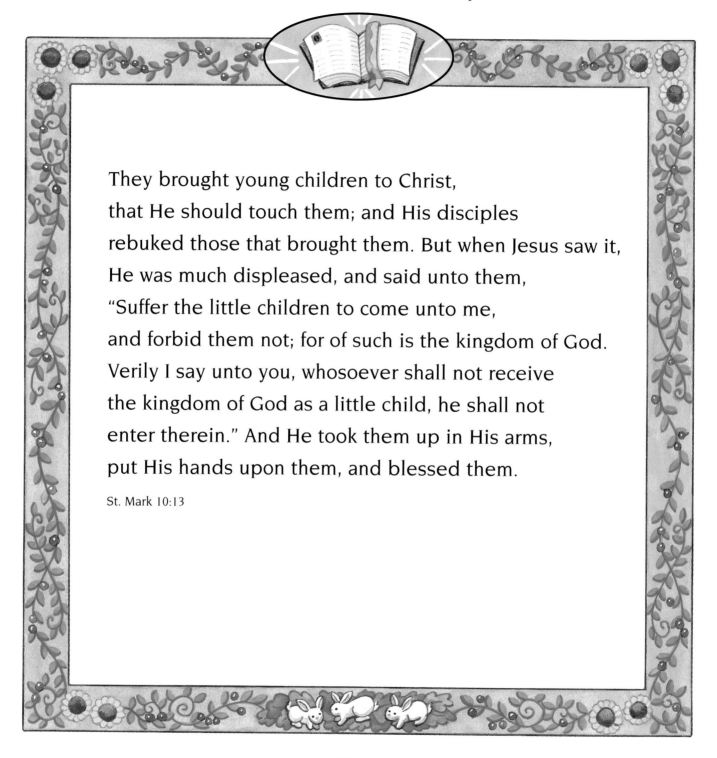

They brought young children to Christ,
that He should touch them; and His disciples
rebuked those that brought them. But when Jesus saw it,
He was much displeased, and said unto them,
"Suffer the little children to come unto me,
and forbid them not; for of such is the kingdom of God.
Verily I say unto you, whosoever shall not receive
the kingdom of God as a little child, he shall not
enter therein." And He took them up in His arms,
put His hands upon them, and blessed them.

St. Mark 10:13

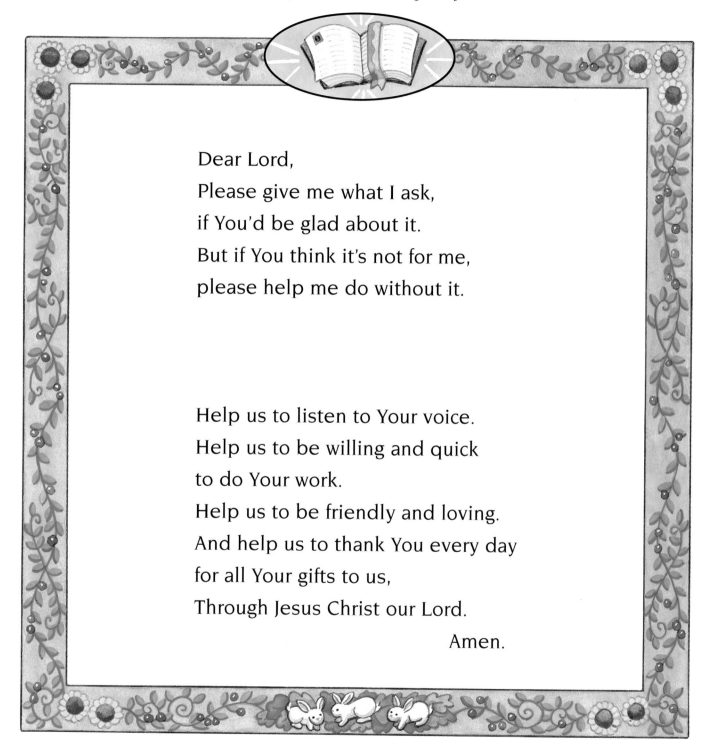

Dear Lord,

Please give me what I ask,

if You'd be glad about it.

But if You think it's not for me,

please help me do without it.

Help us to listen to Your voice.

Help us to be willing and quick

to do Your work.

Help us to be friendly and loving.

And help us to thank You every day

for all Your gifts to us,

Through Jesus Christ our Lord.

Amen.

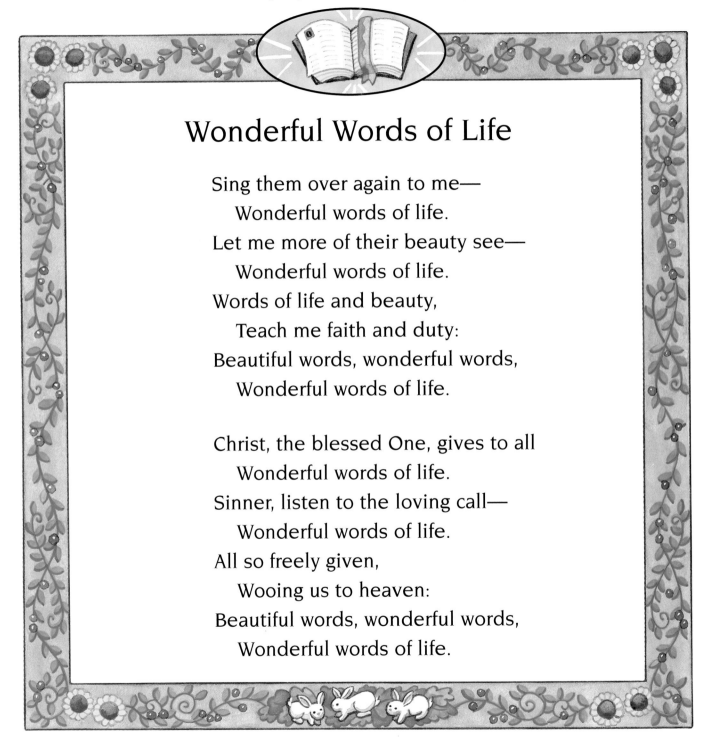

Wonderful Words of Life

Sing them over again to me—
　Wonderful words of life.
Let me more of their beauty see—
　Wonderful words of life.
Words of life and beauty,
　Teach me faith and duty:
Beautiful words, wonderful words,
　Wonderful words of life.

Christ, the blessed One, gives to all
　Wonderful words of life.
Sinner, listen to the loving call—
　Wonderful words of life.
All so freely given,
　Wooing us to heaven:
Beautiful words, wonderful words,
　Wonderful words of life.

Our Father, who art in heaven,
hallowed be Thy name.
Thy kingdom come,
Thy will be done, on earth
as it is in heaven.
Give us this day our daily bread;
and forgive us our trespasses,
as we forgive those who trespass against us;
and lead us not into temptation,
but deliver us from evil.
For Thine is the kingdom,
and the power, and the glory,
for ever and ever.

                                    Amen.

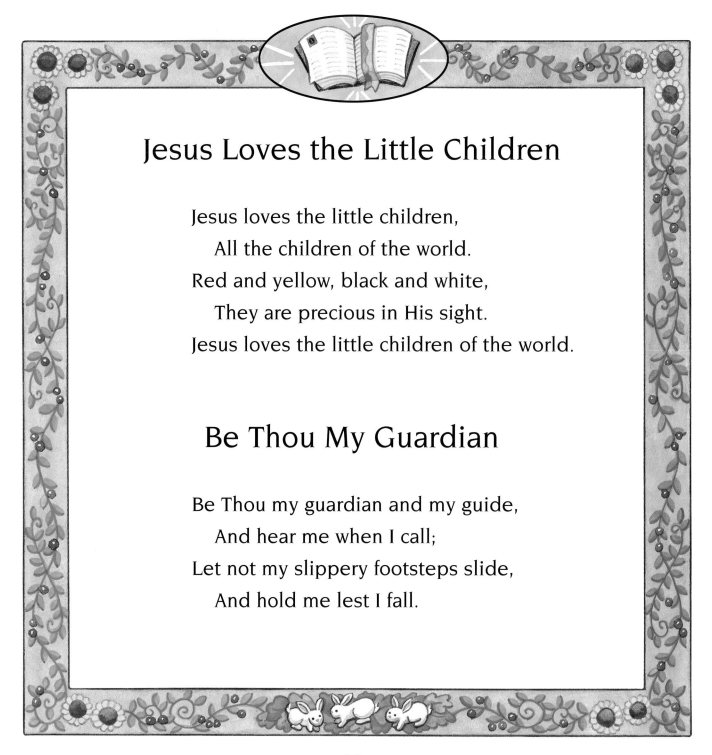

Jesus Loves the Little Children

Jesus loves the little children,
　　All the children of the world.
Red and yellow, black and white,
　　They are precious in His sight.
Jesus loves the little children of the world.

Be Thou My Guardian

Be Thou my guardian and my guide,
　　And hear me when I call;
Let not my slippery footsteps slide,
　　And hold me lest I fall.

Lord, open our eyes,

that we may see You in our brothers and sisters.

Lord, open our ears,

that we may hear the cries of the hungry, the cold,

the frightened, the oppressed.

Lord, open our hearts,

that we may love each other

as You love us.

Renew in us Your spirit,

Lord, free us and make us one.

Mother Teresa

Lord, grant me a simple,

kind, open, believing,

loving, and generous heart,

worthy of being Your dwelling place.

John Sergieff

God be in my head,
and in my understanding.
God be in my eyes,
and in my looking.
God be in my mouth,
and in my speaking.
God be in my heart,
and in my thinking.
God be at my end,
and at my departing.

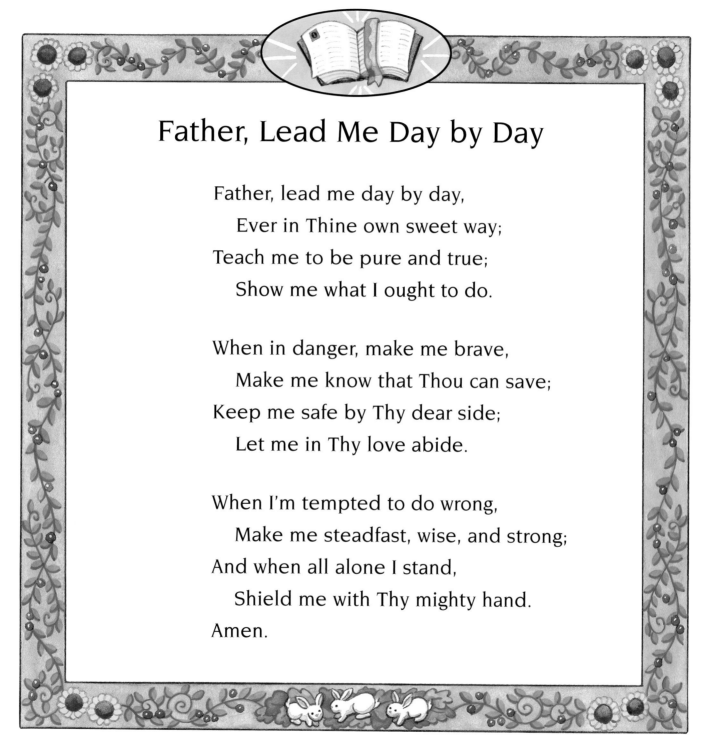

Father, Lead Me Day by Day

Father, lead me day by day,
　　Ever in Thine own sweet way;
Teach me to be pure and true;
　　Show me what I ought to do.

When in danger, make me brave,
　　Make me know that Thou can save;
Keep me safe by Thy dear side;
　　Let me in Thy love abide.

When I'm tempted to do wrong,
　　Make me steadfast, wise, and strong;
And when all alone I stand,
　　Shield me with Thy mighty hand.
Amen.

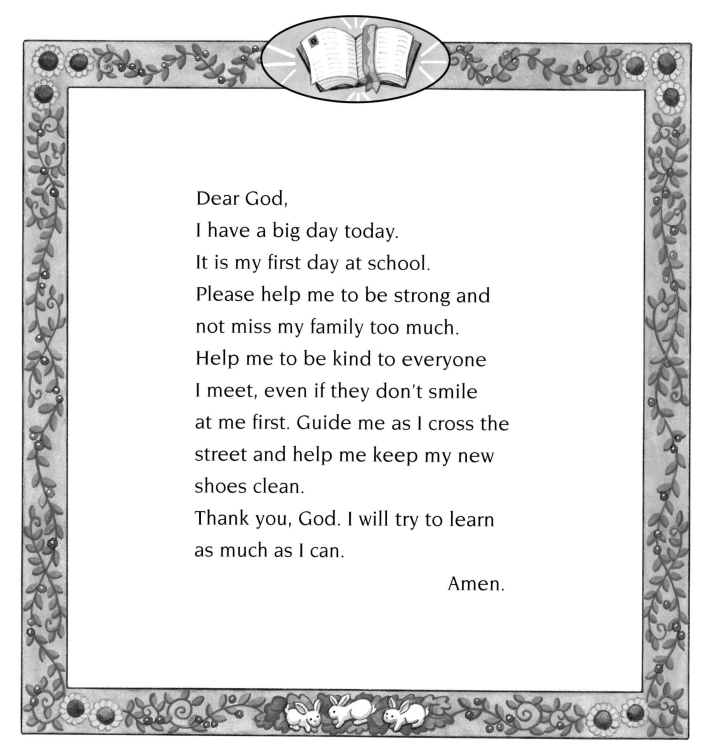

Dear God,

I have a big day today.

It is my first day at school.

Please help me to be strong and
not miss my family too much.
Help me to be kind to everyone
I meet, even if they don't smile
at me first. Guide me as I cross the
street and help me keep my new
shoes clean.

Thank you, God. I will try to learn
as much as I can.

                    Amen.

More Love to Thee

More love to Thee, O Christ,
  More love to Thee!
Hear Thou the prayer I make
  On bended knee;
This is my earnest plea:

More love, O Christ, to Thee,
  More love to Thee,
More love to Thee!

Once earthly joy I craved,
  Sought peace and rest;
Now Thee alone I seek,
  Give what is best;
This all my prayer shall be:

More love, O Christ, to Thee,
  More love to Thee,
More love to Thee!

Dear God,

Be good to me.

The sea is so wide,

and my boat is so small.

All for You, dear God,

everything I do, or think,

or say, the whole day long.

Help me to be good.

I Must Tell Jesus

I must tell Jesus all of my trials,
  I cannot bear these burdens alone;
In my distress He kindly will help me,
  He ever loves and cares for His own.

I must tell Jesus!
  I must tell Jesus!
I cannot bear my burdens alone;
  I must tell Jesus!
I must tell Jesus!
  Jesus can help me, Jesus alone.

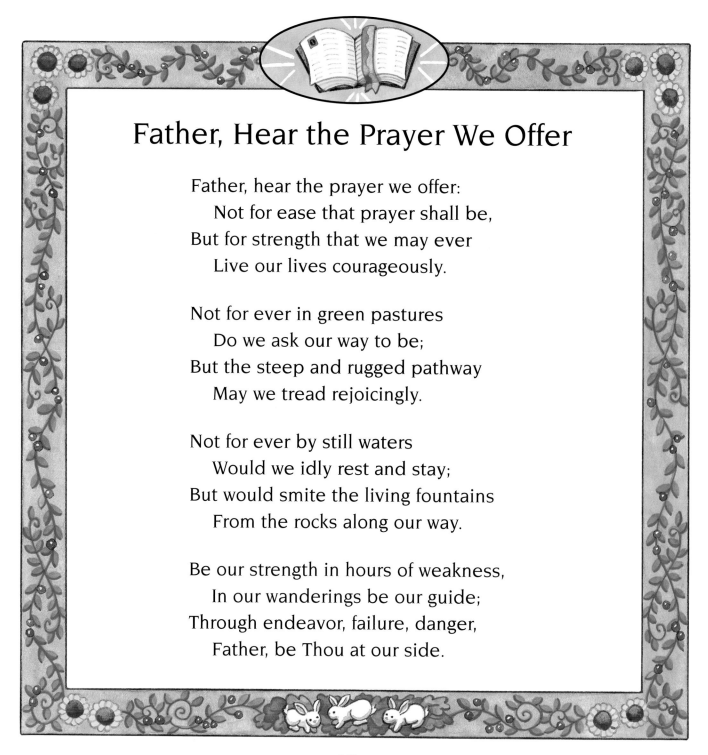

Father, Hear the Prayer We Offer

Father, hear the prayer we offer:
    Not for ease that prayer shall be,
But for strength that we may ever
    Live our lives courageously.

Not for ever in green pastures
    Do we ask our way to be;
But the steep and rugged pathway
    May we tread rejoicingly.

Not for ever by still waters
    Would we idly rest and stay;
But would smite the living fountains
    From the rocks along our way.

Be our strength in hours of weakness,
    In our wanderings be our guide;
Through endeavor, failure, danger,
    Father, be Thou at our side.

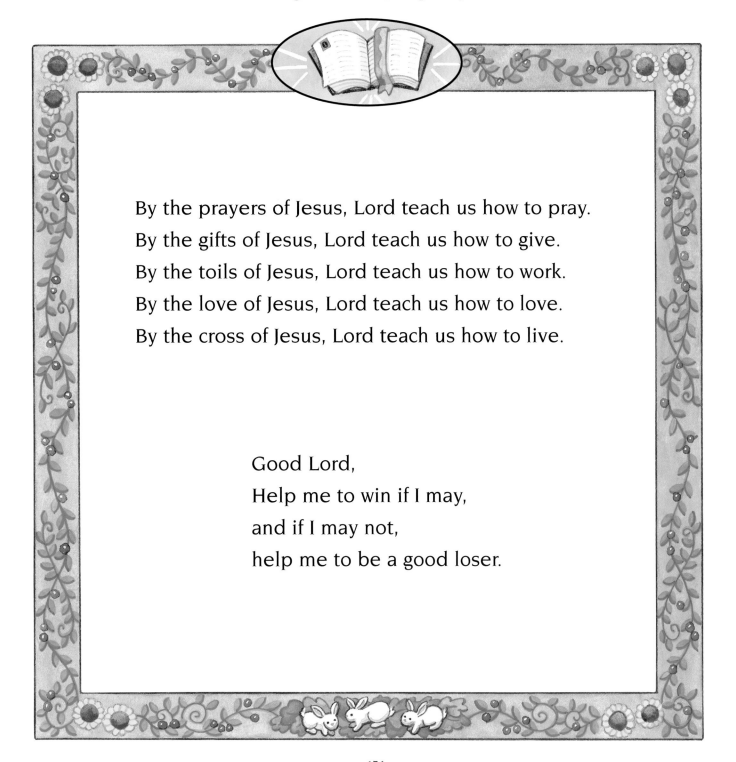

By the prayers of Jesus, Lord teach us how to pray.

By the gifts of Jesus, Lord teach us how to give.

By the toils of Jesus, Lord teach us how to work.

By the love of Jesus, Lord teach us how to love.

By the cross of Jesus, Lord teach us how to live.

Good Lord,

Help me to win if I may,

and if I may not,

help me to be a good loser.

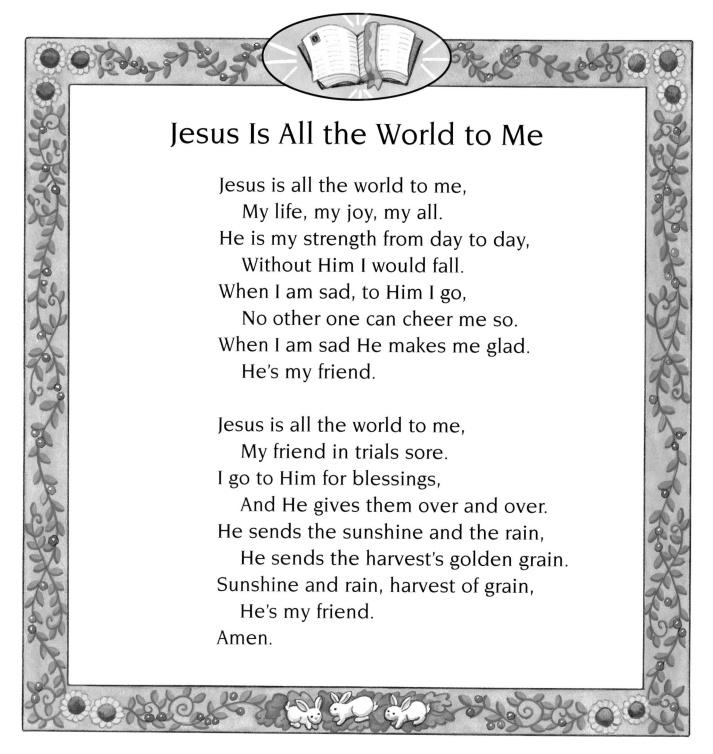

Jesus Is All the World to Me

Jesus is all the world to me,
    My life, my joy, my all.
He is my strength from day to day,
    Without Him I would fall.
When I am sad, to Him I go,
    No other one can cheer me so.
When I am sad He makes me glad.
    He's my friend.

Jesus is all the world to me,
    My friend in trials sore.
I go to Him for blessings,
    And He gives them over and over.
He sends the sunshine and the rain,
    He sends the harvest's golden grain.
Sunshine and rain, harvest of grain,
    He's my friend.
Amen.

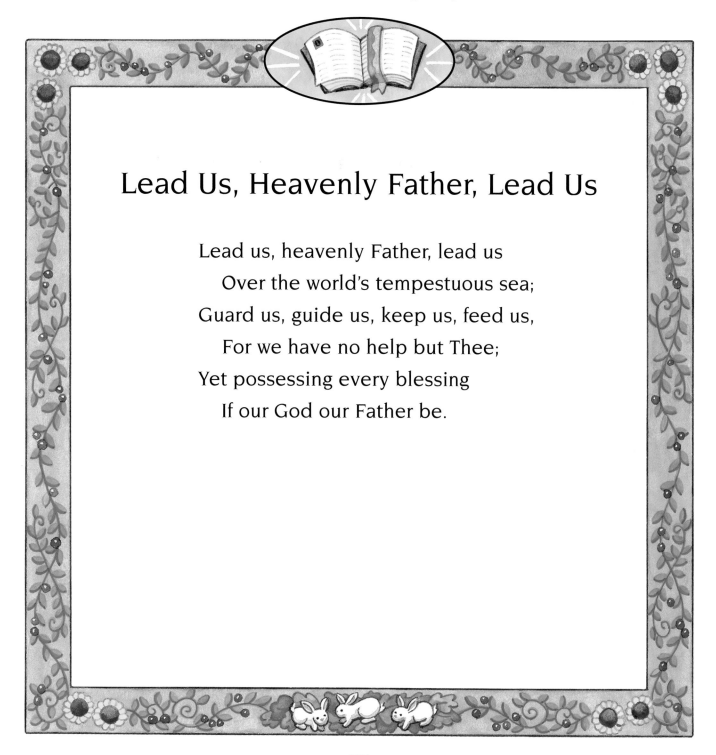

Lead Us, Heavenly Father, Lead Us

Lead us, heavenly Father, lead us
  Over the world's tempestuous sea;
Guard us, guide us, keep us, feed us,
  For we have no help but Thee;
Yet possessing every blessing
  If our God our Father be.

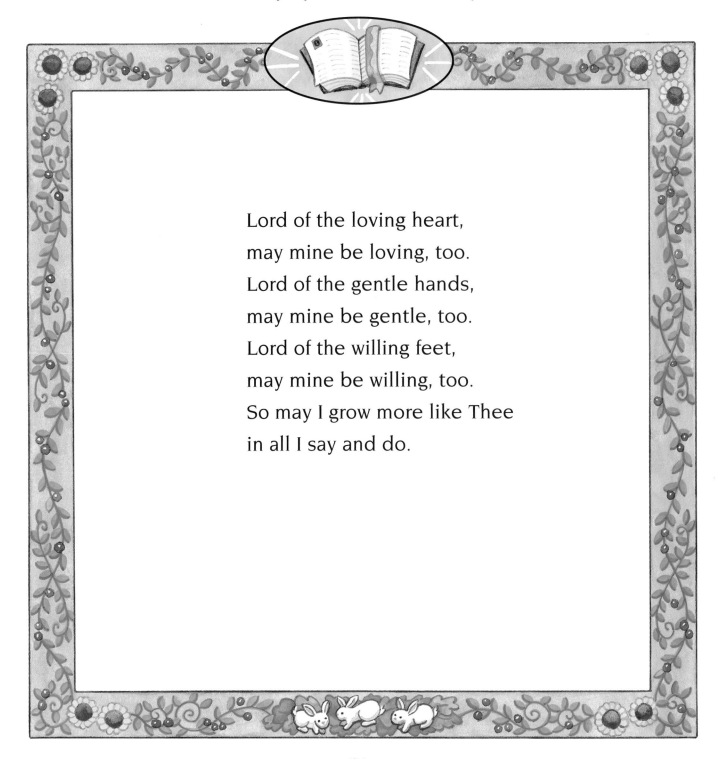

Lord of the loving heart,

may mine be loving, too.

Lord of the gentle hands,

may mine be gentle, too.

Lord of the willing feet,

may mine be willing, too.

So may I grow more like Thee

in all I say and do.

Dear Lord,
Teach this child to pray,
And then accept my prayer.
You hear all the words I say
For You are everywhere.

Jesus Loves Me

O praise Jesus, for He
is with us everywhere.

Sunshine in My Soul

There is sunshine in my soul today,
    More glorious and bright
Than glows in any earthly sky,
    For Jesus is my light.

O there's sunshine, blessed sunshine,
    When the peaceful, happy moments roll;
When Jesus shows His smiling face,
    There is sunshine in my soul.

There is music in my soul today,
    A carol to my King,
And Jesus, listening, can hear
    The songs I cannot sing.

O there's sunshine, blessed sunshine,
    When the peaceful, happy moments roll;
When Jesus shows His smiling face,
    There is sunshine in my soul.

What can I give Him,
    Poor as I am?
If I were a shepherd,
    I would bring a lamb;
If I were a wise man,
    I would do my part;
Yet what can I give Him—
    Give my heart.

Christina Rossetti

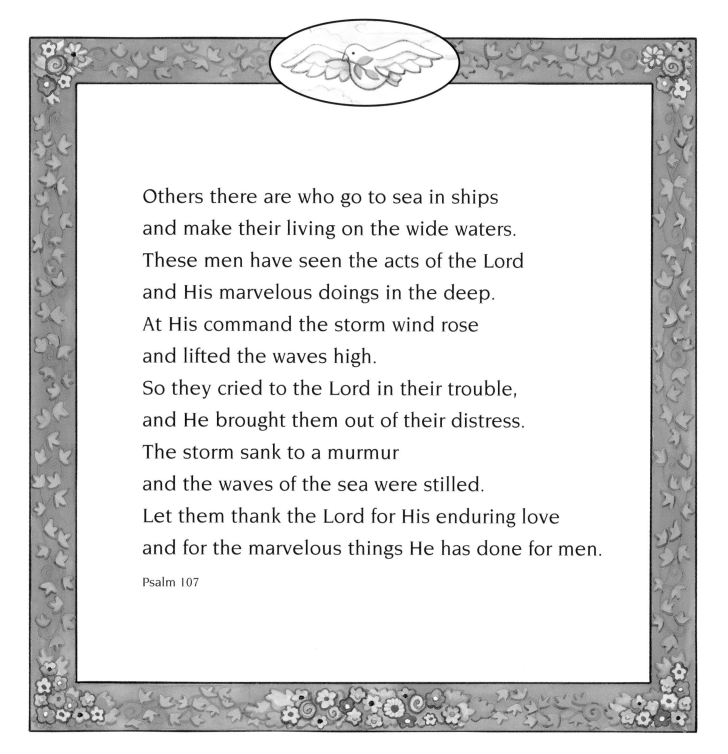

Others there are who go to sea in ships
and make their living on the wide waters.
These men have seen the acts of the Lord
and His marvelous doings in the deep.
At His command the storm wind rose
and lifted the waves high.
So they cried to the Lord in their trouble,
and He brought them out of their distress.
The storm sank to a murmur
and the waves of the sea were stilled.
Let them thank the Lord for His enduring love
and for the marvelous things He has done for men.

Psalm 107

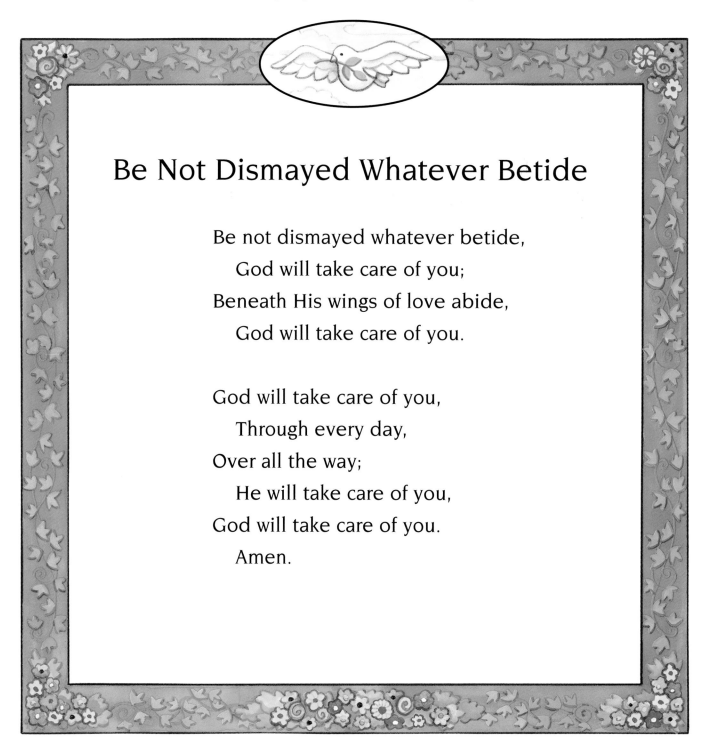

Be Not Dismayed Whatever Betide

Be not dismayed whatever betide,
    God will take care of you;
Beneath His wings of love abide,
    God will take care of you.

God will take care of you,
    Through every day,
Over all the way;
    He will take care of you,
God will take care of you.
    Amen.

Peace Like a River

I've got peace like a river,
I've got peace like a river,
I've got peace like a river in my soul.
I've got peace like a river,
I've got peace like a river,
I've got peace like a river in my soul.

I've got love like an ocean,
I've got love like an ocean,
I've got love like an ocean in my soul.
I've got love like an ocean,
I've got love like an ocean,
I've got love like an ocean in my soul.

I've got joy like a fountain,
I've got joy like a fountain,
I've got joy like a fountain in my soul.
I've got joy like a fountain,
I've got joy like a fountain,
I've got joy like a fountain in my soul.

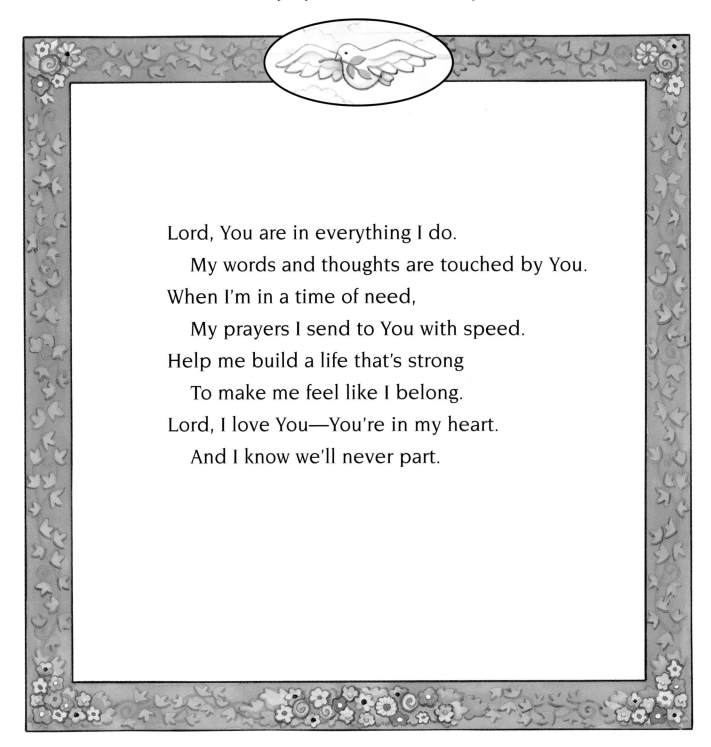

Lord, You are in everything I do.

My words and thoughts are touched by You.

When I'm in a time of need,

My prayers I send to You with speed.

Help me build a life that's strong

To make me feel like I belong.

Lord, I love You—You're in my heart.

And I know we'll never part.

God Moves in a Mysterious Way

God moves in a mysterious way
　　His wonders to perform;
He plants His footsteps in the sea,
　　And rides upon the storm.

Deep in unfathomable mines
　　Of never-failing skill,
He treasures up His bright designs,
　　And works His sovereign will.

Ye fearful saints, fresh courage take,
　　The clouds ye so much dread
Are big with mercy, and shall break
　　In blessings on your head.

Dear Lord,

Thank you for happy summer days.

My friends and I love to splash and play.

We know that You made the pond,

the cattails, and the tickly fishes.

You also made my best friends.

Thank you for each one of them;

each one makes me laugh in his own way.

My friends and I couldn't have

so much fun if it wasn't for You.

Amen.

Every day You bring us joy,
    With puppy dogs and every toy.
In each and every friendship, too,
    We feel the strength and love of You.
Lord, how You touch our lives,
    Our faith and love keeps us alive.

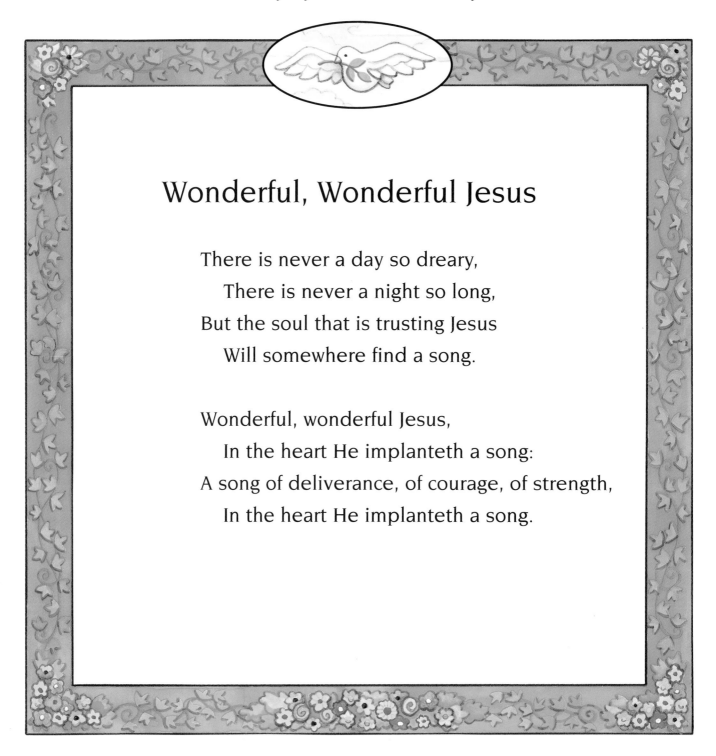

Wonderful, Wonderful Jesus

There is never a day so dreary,
  There is never a night so long,
But the soul that is trusting Jesus
  Will somewhere find a song.

Wonderful, wonderful Jesus,
  In the heart He implanteth a song:
A song of deliverance, of courage, of strength,
  In the heart He implanteth a song.

What a Friend We Have in Jesus

What a friend we have in Jesus,
All our sins and griefs to bear,
What a privilege to carry
Everything to God in prayer.

O what peace we often forfeit,
O what needless pain we bear,
All because we do not carry
Everything to God in prayer.

Praise Him, All Ye Little Children

Praise Him, praise Him, all ye little children;
   God is Love, God is Love.
Praise Him, praise Him, all ye little children;
   God is Love, God is Love.

Love Him, love Him, all ye little children;
   God is Love, God is Love.
Love Him, love Him, all ye little children;
   God is Love, God is Love.

Serve Him, serve Him, all ye little children;
   God is Love, God is Love.
Serve Him, serve Him, all ye little children;
   God is Love, God is Love.

The Name of Jesus

The name of Jesus is so sweet,
  I love its music to repeat.
It makes my joys full and complete,
  The precious name of Jesus.

"Jesus," O how sweet the name!
  "Jesus," every day the same.
"Jesus," let all saints proclaim
  Its worthy praise forever.

I love the name of Him whose heart
  Knows all my griefs, and bears a part,
Who bids all anxious fears depart.
  I love the name of Jesus.

"Jesus," O how sweet the name!
  "Jesus," every day the same.
"Jesus," let all saints proclaim
  Its worthy praise forever.

O praise God in His holiness; praise Him in the firmament of His power.

Praise Him in His noble acts; praise Him according to His excellent greatness.

Praise Him in the sound of the trumpet; praise Him upon the lute and harp.

Praise Him in the cymbals and dances; praise Him upon the strings and pipe.

Praise Him upon the well-tuned cymbals; praise Him upon the loud cymbals.

Let everything that hath breath praise the Lord.

Psalm 150

Praise to the Lord, the Almighty

Praise to the Lord, the Almighty,
  The King of creation;
O my soul, praise Him,
  For He is thy health and salvation.
Come, ye who hear,
  Brothers and sisters, draw near,
Praise Him in glad adoration.

O for a Closer Walk With God

O for a closer walk with God,
  A calm and heavenly frame;
A light to shine upon the road
  That leads me to the Lamb!

There Is a Land of Pure Delight

There is a land of pure delight
　　Where saints immortal reign;
Infinite day excludes the night,
　　And pleasures banish pain.

There everlasting spring abides,
　　And never-withering flowers;
Death, like a narrow sea, divides
　　This heavenly land from ours.

A Shelter in the Time of Storm

The Lord's our Rock, in Him we hide—
    A shelter in the time of storm;
Secure whatever ill betide—
    A shelter in the time of storm.

O Jesus is a Rock in a weary land,
    A weary land, a weary land;
O Jesus is a Rock in a weary land—
    A shelter in the time of storm.

A shade by day, defense by night—
    A shelter in the time of storm;
No fears alarm, no foes affright—
    A shelter in the time of storm.

O Jesus is a Rock in a weary land,
    A weary land, a weary land;
O Jesus is a Rock in a weary land—
    A shelter in the time of storm.

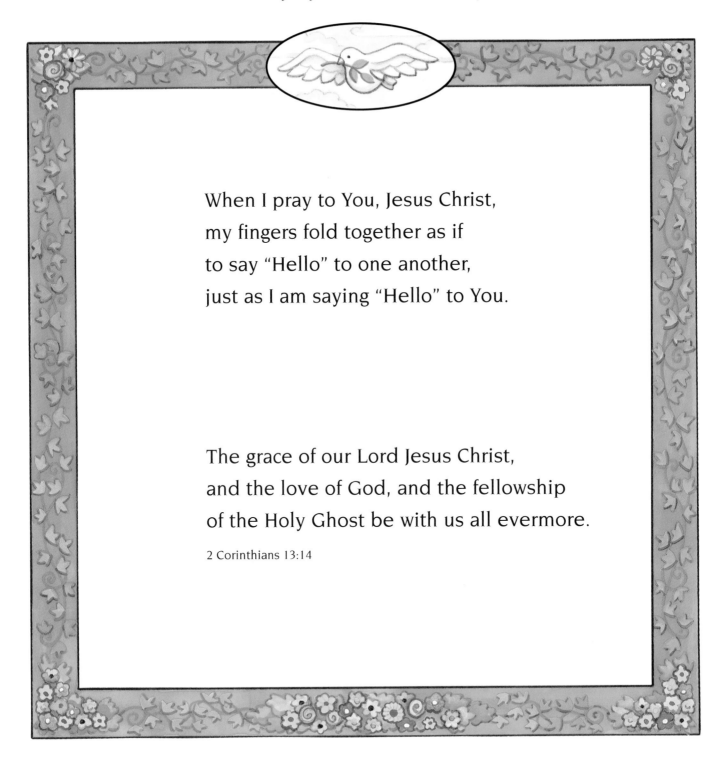

When I pray to You, Jesus Christ,
my fingers fold together as if
to say "Hello" to one another,
just as I am saying "Hello" to You.

The grace of our Lord Jesus Christ,
and the love of God, and the fellowship
of the Holy Ghost be with us all evermore.

2 Corinthians 13:14

God is Light:
and in Him is no darkness at all.

God is not far from every one of us:
in Him we live and move and have our being.

The peace of God, which passeth
all understanding, keep your hearts
and minds in the knowledge and
love of God, and of His Son, Jesus Christ
our Lord: And the blessing of God Almighty,
the Father, the Son, and the Holy Ghost,
be amongst you and remain with you always.

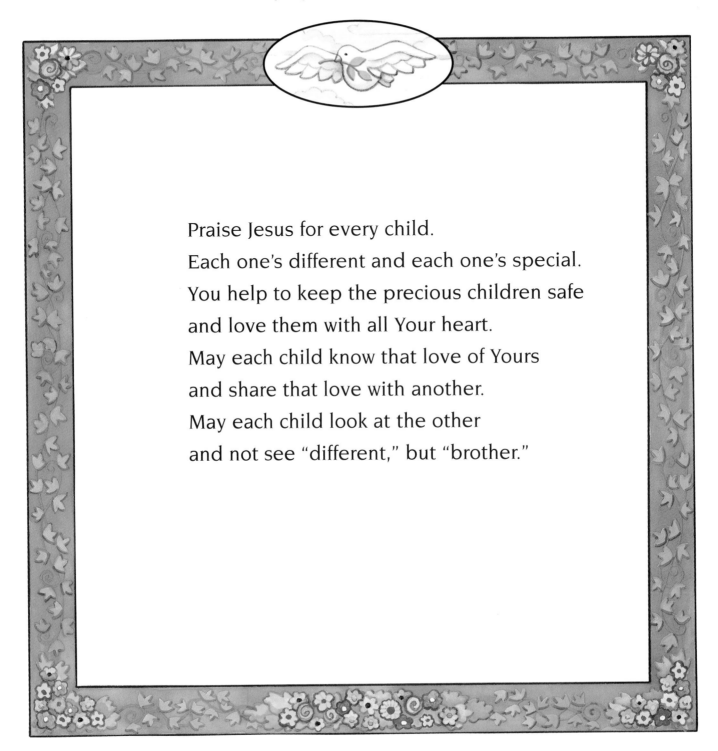

Praise Jesus for every child.

Each one's different and each one's special.

You help to keep the precious children safe

and love them with all Your heart.

May each child know that love of Yours

and share that love with another.

May each child look at the other

and not see "different," but "brother."

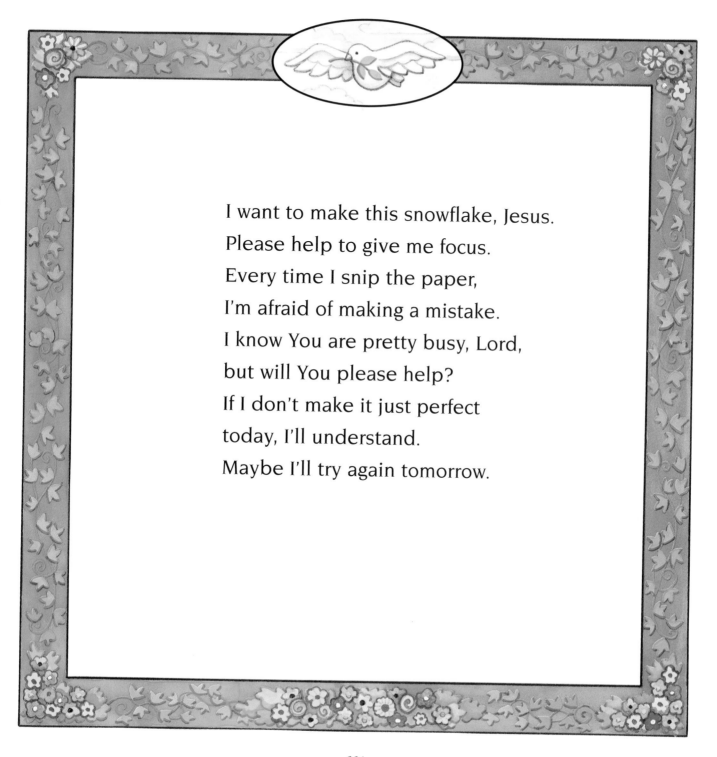

I want to make this snowflake, Jesus.

Please help to give me focus.

Every time I snip the paper,

I'm afraid of making a mistake.

I know You are pretty busy, Lord,

but will You please help?

If I don't make it just perfect

today, I'll understand.

Maybe I'll try again tomorrow.

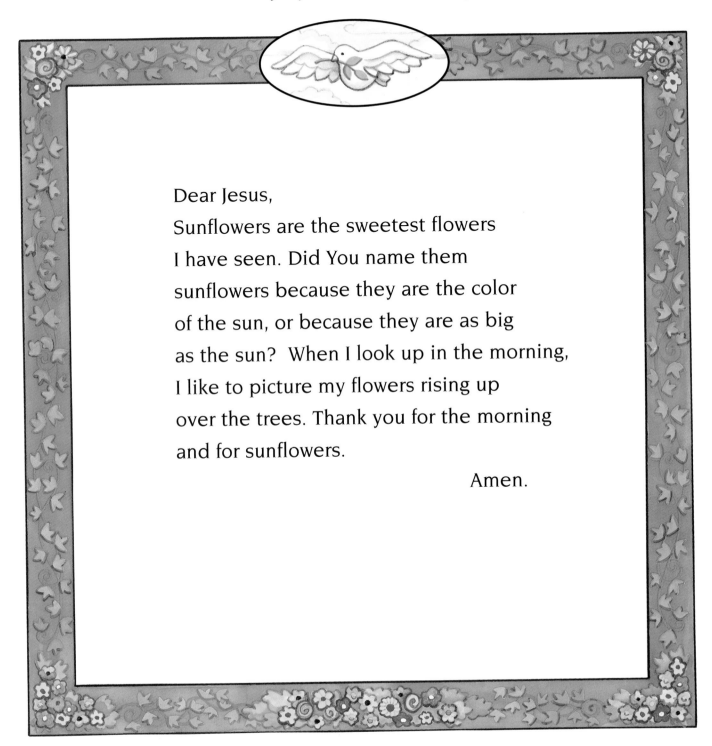

Dear Jesus,

Sunflowers are the sweetest flowers
I have seen. Did You name them
sunflowers because they are the color
of the sun, or because they are as big
as the sun? When I look up in the morning,
I like to picture my flowers rising up
over the trees. Thank you for the morning
and for sunflowers.

Amen.

There is no Holy One like the Lord;
there is no one besides You;
there is no Rock like our God.

1 Samuel 2:2

The World Around Me

The love of God is shown
in the beauty of the earth.

Dear God,

I'm glad the sky is painted blue,

And the earth is painted green,

With such a lot of nice fresh air

All sandwiched in-between.

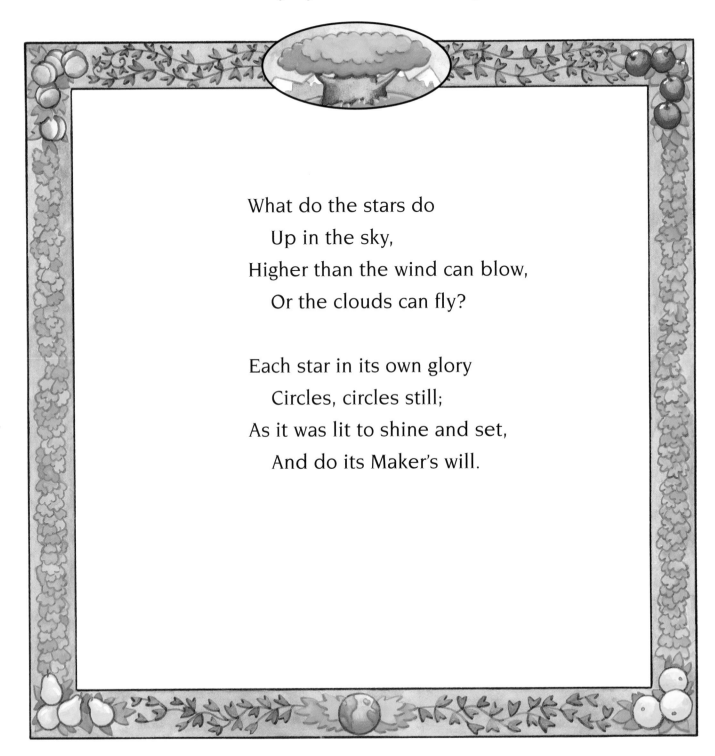

What do the stars do
   Up in the sky,
Higher than the wind can blow,
   Or the clouds can fly?

Each star in its own glory
   Circles, circles still;
As it was lit to shine and set,
   And do its Maker's will.

For rosy apples, juicy plums,

And yellow pears so sweet,

For hips and haws on bush and hedge,

And flowers at our feet,

For ears of corn all ripe and dry,

And colored leaves on trees,

We thank You, heavenly Jesus Christ,

For such good gifts as these.

Out in the Fields

The little cares that worried me,
   I lost them yesterday
Among the fields above the sea,
   Among the lowing of the herds,
The rustling of the trees,
   Among the singing of the birds,
The humming of the bees.

The foolish fears of what might pass,
   I cast them all away
Among the clover-scented grass,
   Among the new-mown hay,
Among the hushing of the corn,
   Where drowsy poppies nod,
Where ill thoughts die and good are born—
   Out in the fields of God.

I Never Saw a Moor

I never saw a moor,
   I never saw the sea;
Yet know I how the heather looks,
   And what a wave must be.

I never spoke with God,
   Nor visited in heaven;
Yet certain am I of the spot
   As if the chart were given.

Emily Dickinson

Dear Jesus,

Who has made all things beautiful:

give me a love of Thy countryside, its lanes

and meadows, its woods and streams, and

clean open spaces; and let me keep it fresh and

unspoiled for those who shall come after me.

Amen.

Keep us, O Lord, as the apple of Your eye;

hide us under the shadow of Your wings.

When the weather is wet,
  We must not fret.
When the weather is cold,
  We must not scold.
When the weather is warm,
  We must not storm.
Be thankful together,
  Whatever the weather.

In the Garden

I come to the garden alone,
    While the dew is still on the roses.
And the voice I hear,
    Falling on my ear,
The Son of God discloses.

And He walks with me,
    And He talks with me,
And He tells me I am His own.
    And the joy we share
As we tarry there,
    None other has ever known.

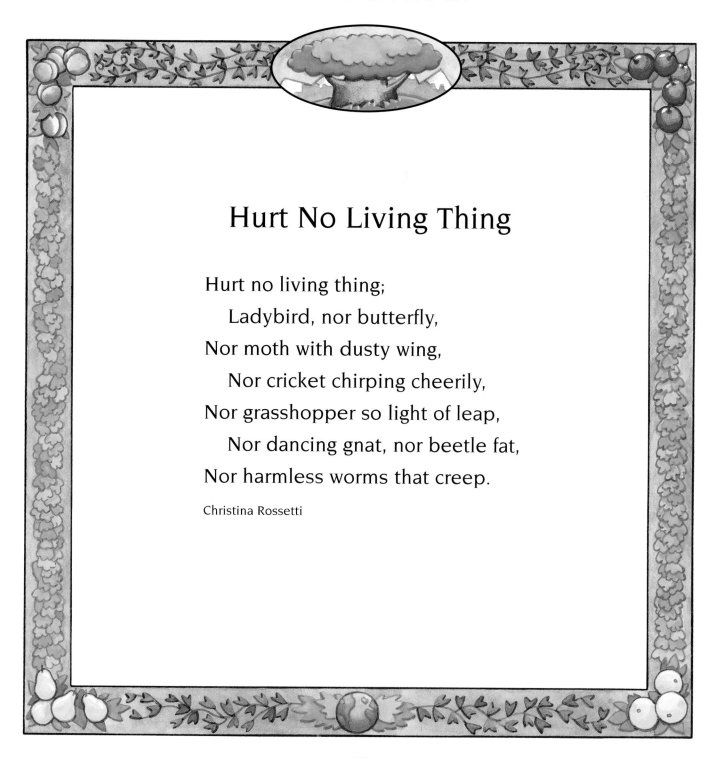

Hurt No Living Thing

Hurt no living thing;
   Ladybird, nor butterfly,
Nor moth with dusty wing,
   Nor cricket chirping cheerily,
Nor grasshopper so light of leap,
   Nor dancing gnat, nor beetle fat,
Nor harmless worms that creep.

Christina Rossetti

God bless the field and bless the lane,
Stream and branch and lion's mane,
Hill and stone and flower and tree,
From every end of my country—
Bless the sun and bless the sleet,
Bless the road and bless the street,
Bless the night and bless the day,
In each and every tiny way;
Bless the minnow, bless the whale,
Bless the rainbow and the hail,
Bless the nest and bless the leaf,
Bless the righteous and the thief,
Bless the wing and bless the fin,
Bless the air I travel in,
Bless the mill and bless the mouse,
Bless the miller's bricken house,
Bless the earth and bless the sea,
God bless you and God bless me.

Jesus Shall Reign Wherever the Sun

Jesus shall reign wherever the sun
    Does His successive journeys run;
His kingdom stretch from shore to shore
    Till moons shall wax and wane no more.
Let every creature rise and bring
    Peculiar honors to our King;
Angels descend with songs again,
    And earth repeat the long amen.

Enjoy all of creation,
each leaf and flower and every small
pebble along the way.
Embrace the hope of each new morning,
and the last ray of sunshine
to fall at day's end.

Anna Trimiew

For the Beauty of the Earth

For the beauty of the earth,
    For the glory of the skies,
For the love which from our birth
    Over and around us lies:
Christ our God, to Thee we raise
    This our hymn of grateful praise.

For the wonder of each hour
    Of the day and of the night,
Hill and vale and tree and flower,
    Sun and moon and stars of light:
Christ our God, to Thee we raise
    This our hymn of grateful praise.

Thank God for rain
and the beautiful rainbow colors.
And thank God for letting children
splash in puddles.

The Lord is good to me,
and so I thank the Lord
for giving me the things I need:
the sun, the rain, and the apple seed!
The Lord is good to me.

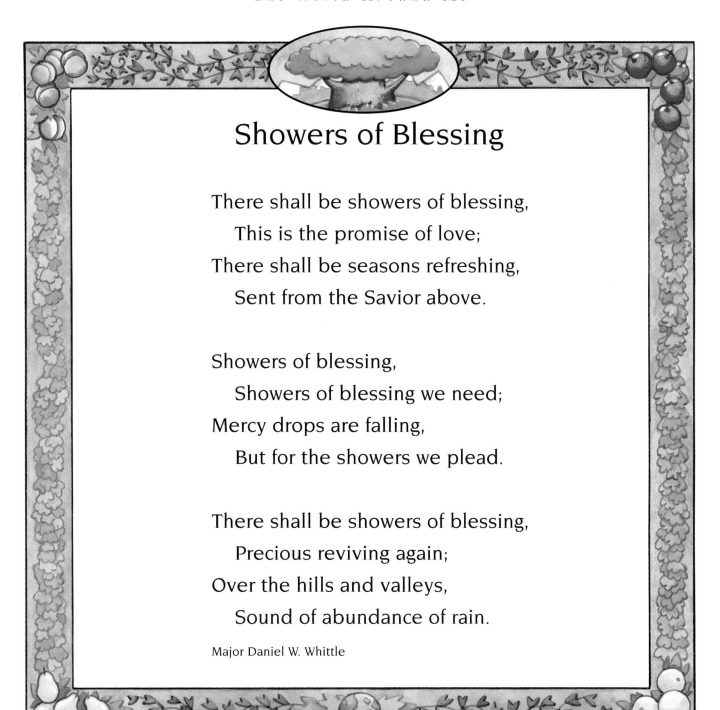

Showers of Blessing

There shall be showers of blessing,
This is the promise of love;
There shall be seasons refreshing,
Sent from the Savior above.

Showers of blessing,
Showers of blessing we need;
Mercy drops are falling,
But for the showers we plead.

There shall be showers of blessing,
Precious reviving again;
Over the hills and valleys,
Sound of abundance of rain.

Major Daniel W. Whittle

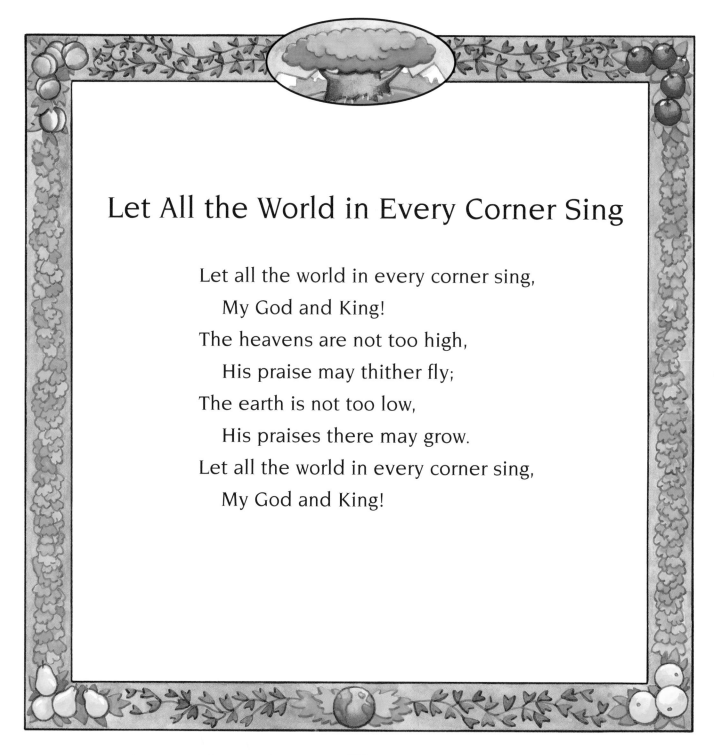

Let All the World in Every Corner Sing

Let all the world in every corner sing,
    My God and King!
The heavens are not too high,
    His praise may thither fly;
The earth is not too low,
    His praises there may grow.
Let all the world in every corner sing,
    My God and King!

Pied Beauty

Glory be to God for dappled things—
    For skies of couple-color as a brindled cow;
For rose-moles all in stipple upon trout that swim;
    Fresh-firecoal chestnut-falls; finches' wings;
Landscape plotted and pieced—fold, fallow, and plough;
    And all trades, their gear and tackle and trim.

All things counter, original, spare, strange;
    Whatever is fickle, freckled (who knows how?)
With swift, slow; sweet, sour; adazzle, dim;
    He fathers-forth whose beauty is past change:
Praise Him.

Gerard Manley Hopkins

Music is the art of the prophets,
the only art that can calm the
agitations of the soul: it is one
of the most magnificent and delightful
presents God has given us.

Martin Luther

God made the sun,
    And God made the trees.
God made the mountains,
    And God made me.

Thank you, O God,
    For the sun and the trees,
For making the mountains,
    And for making me.

All People That on Earth Do Dwell

All people that on earth do dwell,
    Sing to the Lord with cheerful voice;
Him serve with mirth, His praise forth tell,
    Come ye before Him, and rejoice.

The Lord, ye know, is God indeed;
    Without our aid He did us make;
We are His folk, He doth us feed,
    And for His sheep He doth us take.

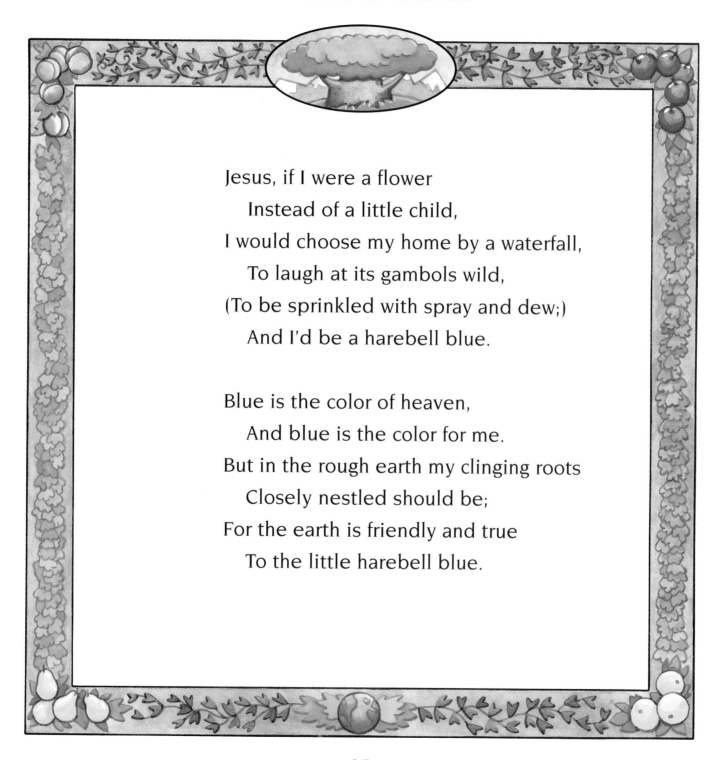

Jesus, if I were a flower
   Instead of a little child,
I would choose my home by a waterfall,
   To laugh at its gambols wild,
(To be sprinkled with spray and dew;)
   And I'd be a harebell blue.

Blue is the color of heaven,
   And blue is the color for me.
But in the rough earth my clinging roots
   Closely nestled should be;
For the earth is friendly and true
   To the little harebell blue.

Father, We Thank Thee

For flowers that bloom about our feet,
    Father, we thank Thee,
For tender grass so fresh and sweet,
    Father, we thank Thee,
For the song of bird and hum of bee,
    For all things fair we hear or see,
Father in heaven, we thank Thee.

(continued)

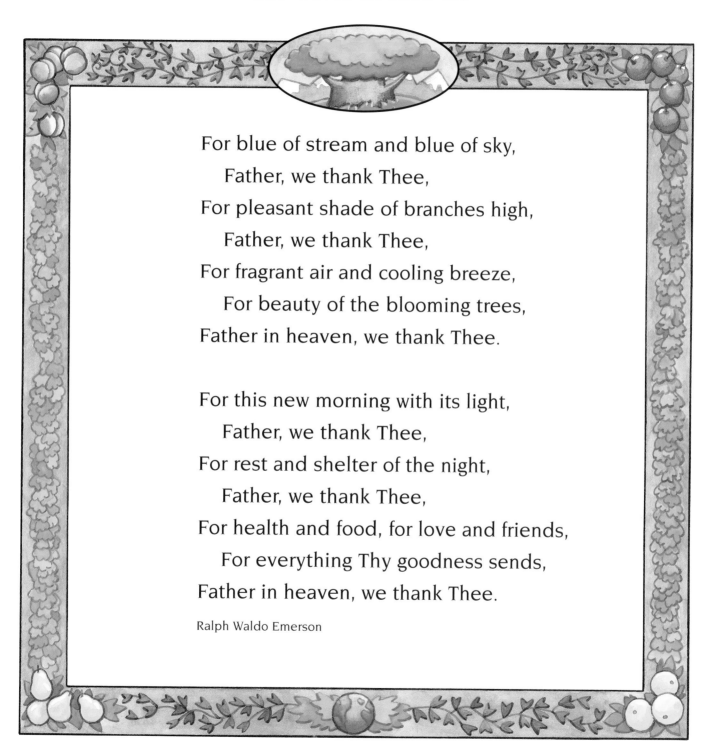

For blue of stream and blue of sky,
  Father, we thank Thee,
For pleasant shade of branches high,
  Father, we thank Thee,
For fragrant air and cooling breeze,
  For beauty of the blooming trees,
Father in heaven, we thank Thee.

For this new morning with its light,
  Father, we thank Thee,
For rest and shelter of the night,
  Father, we thank Thee,
For health and food, for love and friends,
  For everything Thy goodness sends,
Father in heaven, we thank Thee.

Ralph Waldo Emerson

The trees are shedding all their leaves,
    Soon it will grow colder.
O dear Jesus, be with me—
    Your love wrapped round my shoulder.

As You keep me snuggled tight,
    I'll sit and watch the trees.
For they might get chilled at night,
    Without their blankets green.

When to the flowers so beautiful
the Father gave a name,
Back came a little blue-eyed one,
all timidly she came.
And standing at the Father's feet
and gazing in His face
She said in low and trembling tones,
"Dear God, the name Thou gave to me,
alas, I have forgot."
Then kindly looked the Father down
and said, "Forget Me not."

Every Creature Great and Small

Fuzzy, feathered, or finned,
Jesus loves every creature.

The birds above me,

the kitten on my lap,

the toad that hops,

the deer that runs,

Lord Jesus, it was You who

created all these wonderful animals.

Thank you, Lord.

They are treasured.

Something so tiny as a butterfly
can hold all the love of Jesus.

Praise God, from whom all blessings flow!
Praise Him, all creatures here below!
Praise Him above, ye heavenly Host!
Praise Father, Son, and Holy Ghost.

If a rabbit had words,

it would thank You for its ears.

If an elephant had words,

it would thank You for its trunk.

If a zebra had words,

it would thank You for its stripes.

If a cat had words,

it would thank You for its whiskers.

But since only I have words, dear Jesus,

I will thank You for them all!

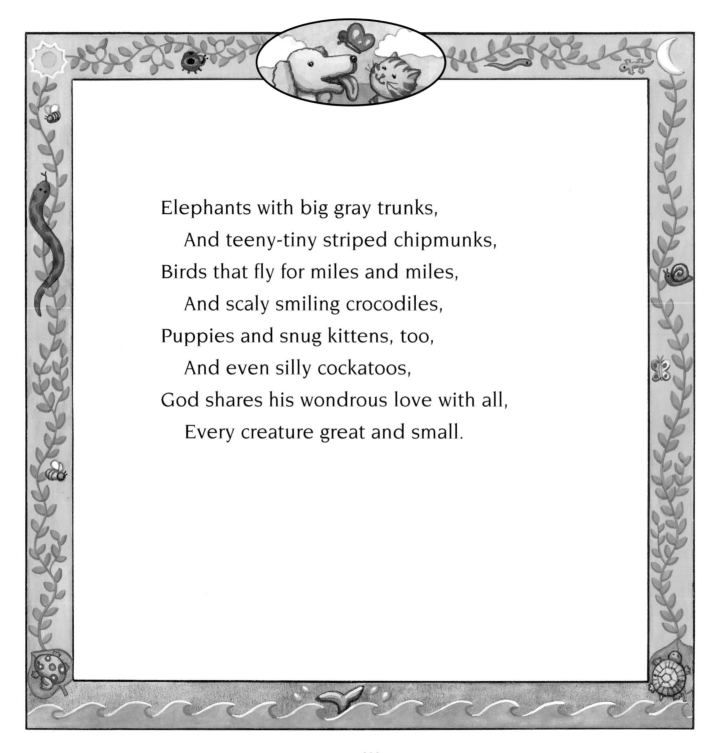

Elephants with big gray trunks,
    And teeny-tiny striped chipmunks,
Birds that fly for miles and miles,
    And scaly smiling crocodiles,
Puppies and snug kittens, too,
    And even silly cockatoos,
God shares his wondrous love with all,
    Every creature great and small.

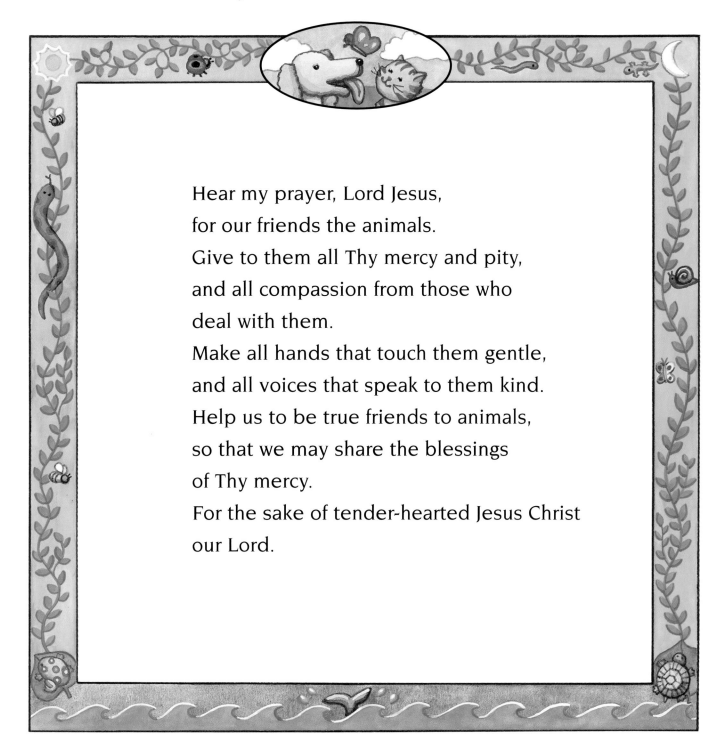

Hear my prayer, Lord Jesus,
for our friends the animals.
Give to them all Thy mercy and pity,
and all compassion from those who
deal with them.
Make all hands that touch them gentle,
and all voices that speak to them kind.
Help us to be true friends to animals,
so that we may share the blessings
of Thy mercy.
For the sake of tender-hearted Jesus Christ
our Lord.

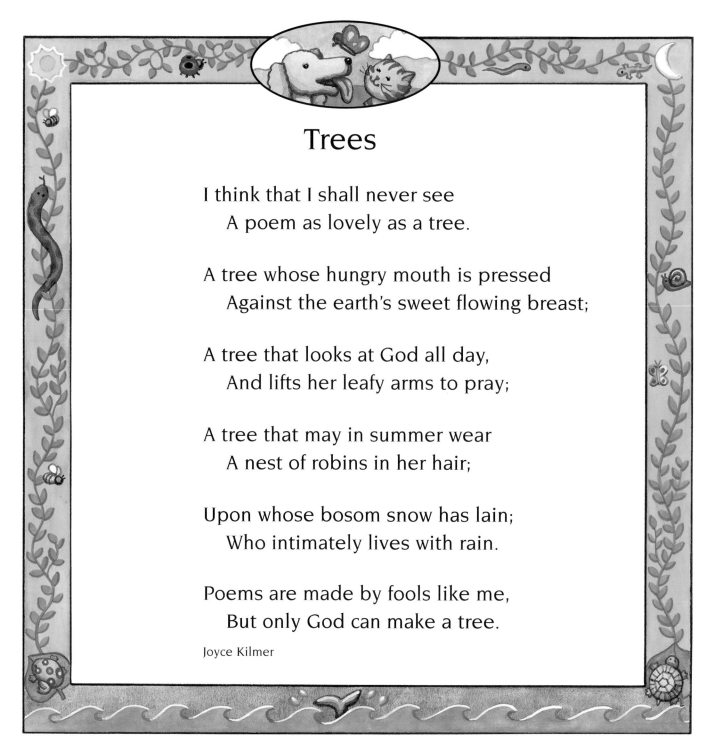

Trees

I think that I shall never see
    A poem as lovely as a tree.

A tree whose hungry mouth is pressed
    Against the earth's sweet flowing breast;

A tree that looks at God all day,
    And lifts her leafy arms to pray;

A tree that may in summer wear
    A nest of robins in her hair;

Upon whose bosom snow has lain;
    Who intimately lives with rain.

Poems are made by fools like me,
    But only God can make a tree.

Joyce Kilmer

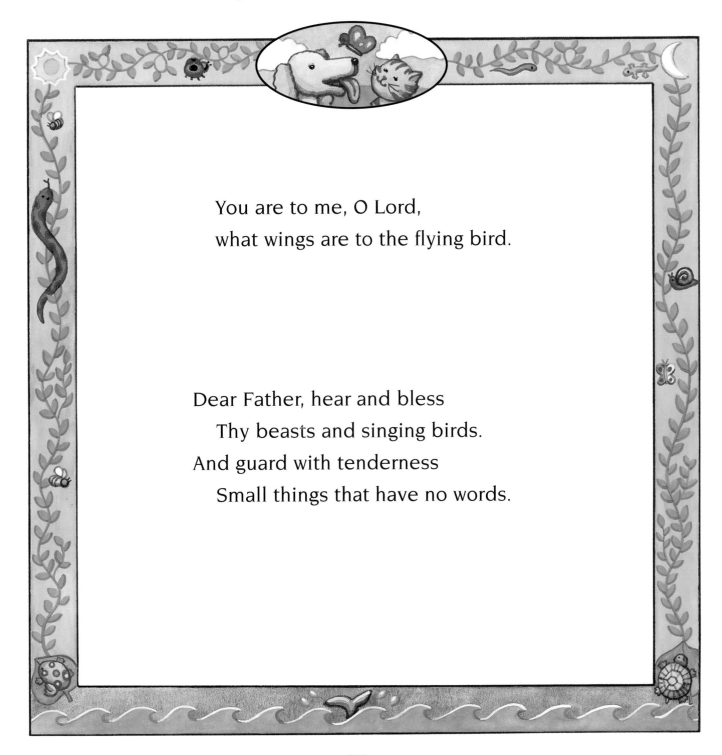

You are to me, O Lord,
what wings are to the flying bird.

Dear Father, hear and bless
Thy beasts and singing birds.
And guard with tenderness
Small things that have no words.

My kitten is so warm and snug,
Whether on the windowsill or rug.
I love to watch her night and day
And for her safety, Lord, I pray.

Thank you, God, for the warm
snuggles of my kitten.

The Lamb

Little lamb, who made thee?
   Dost thou know who made thee;
Gave thee life and bid thee feed
   By the stream and over the mead;
Gave thee clothing of delight,
   Softest clothing, woolly, bright;
Gave thee such a tender voice
   Making all the vales rejoice?
Little lamb, who made thee?
   Dost thou know who made thee?

(continued)

Little lamb, I'll tell thee,
    Little lamb, I'll tell thee:
He is called by thy name,
    For He calls Himself a Lamb.
He is meek and He is mild;
    He became a little child.
I a child and thou a lamb,
    We are called by His name.
Little lamb, God bless thee.
    Little lamb, God bless thee.

William Blake

A tiny egg is about to hatch
while a mother bluebird waits
to meet her baby for the first time.
Thank you, Lord,
for nature's miracles.

Dear Jesus,
Sometimes all I need to do is
look at my dog watching me,
and I know I am being taken care of,
in more ways than one.

Lord Jesus,
Bless my tiny puppy
as he sits at home all day.
For he is so brave and believes himself
to be a great watchdog, while still so small.

All things bright and beautiful,
All creatures great and small,
All things wise and wonderful,
The Lord God made them all.

Cecil Frances Alexander

Whether with my puppy or my teddy bear,
I know I'm loved and You are here.
Thank you, Lord, for my best friends,
And thank you for the love You send.

He prayeth best, who loveth best
All things both great and small;
For the dear God who loveth us,
He made and loveth all.

A Friend Is Love

A friend, like Jesus,
loves unconditionally.

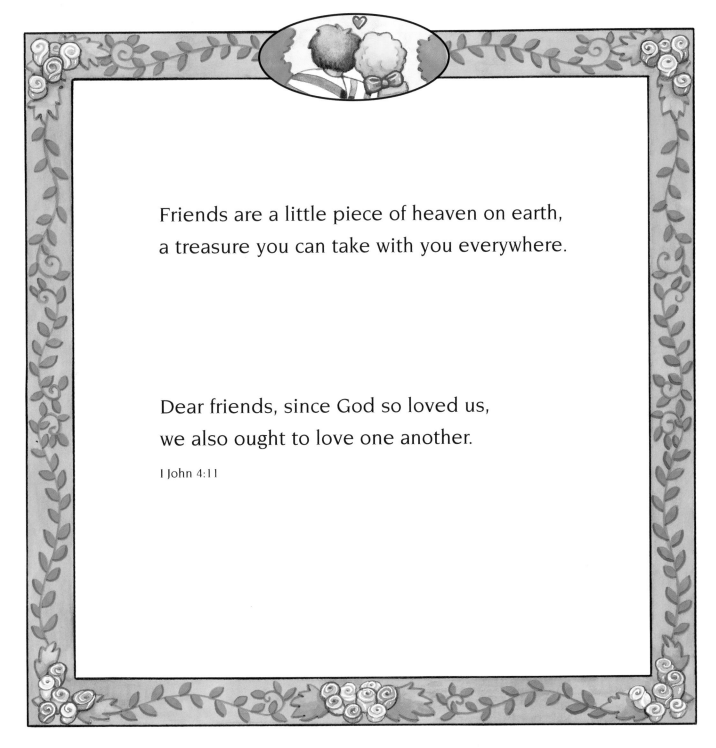

Friends are a little piece of heaven on earth,
a treasure you can take with you everywhere.

Dear friends, since God so loved us,
we also ought to love one another.

I John 4:11

A friend is someone who doesn't judge.

A friend is someone who loves me for me.

A friend can play and make me happy,

but a friend also understands when I can't play.

You are my friend, Jesus.

Thank you for being my friend.

Lord Jesus Christ,
Teach me the ways of friendship
so that I may be a good friend
to someone who needs me,
just like You.

My friend is special to me.
Lord Jesus, please help me to
keep her in my heart until we grow old.

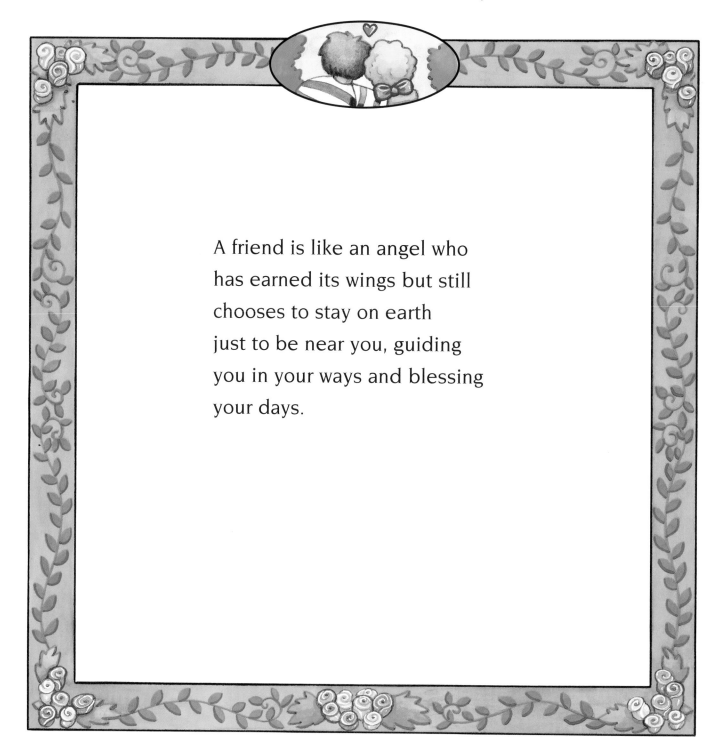

A friend is like an angel who
has earned its wings but still
chooses to stay on earth
just to be near you, guiding
you in your ways and blessing
your days.

Friendship always shines on a cloudy day,

Sending rainbows to guide your way.

Bright colors of joy painted with love,

A friend is a blessing from above.

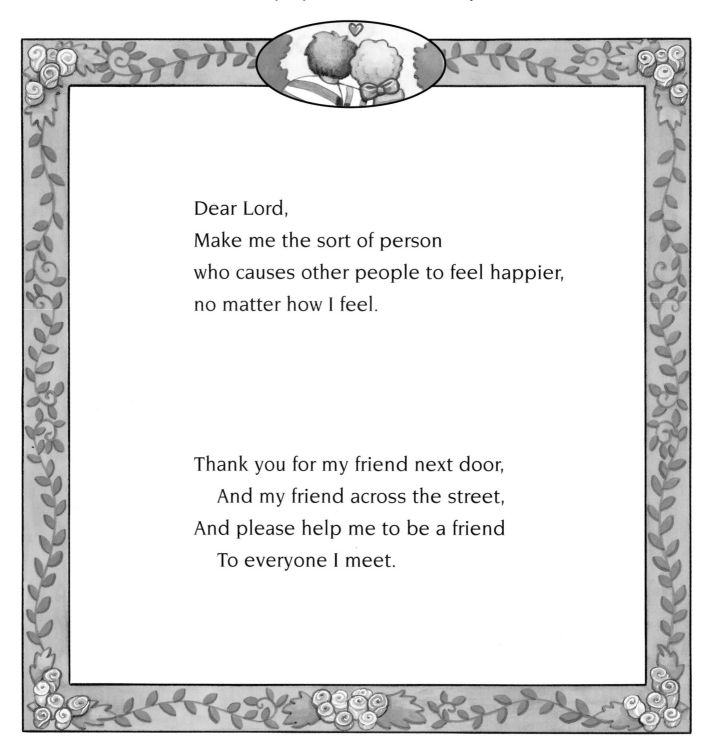

Dear Lord,
Make me the sort of person
who causes other people to feel happier,
no matter how I feel.

Thank you for my friend next door,
    And my friend across the street,
And please help me to be a friend
    To everyone I meet.

Now I lay me down to sleep.

I pray Thee, Lord, my soul to keep.

Your love be with me through the night

And wake me with the morning light.

Lord, keep us safe this night,

Secure from all our fears.

May angels guard us while we sleep,

Till morning light appears.